AF264466

iv

Reviews

"Takara speaks of the volcano as though she knows it. I do too. I witnessed the 1959 birth of this volcano within a volcano. For the first time, in reading Kathryn's newest book, I feel my experience has been truly described. Kathryn's innate talent at storytelling makes ***Red Dreams, Volcano Visions*** a compelling reading companion."

> — Alexandra Avery,
> author,
> aromatherapist

"Kathryn, I am so glad I read your book, ***Red Dreams, Volcano Visions***. I found your artistic blend of legend, present-day stories, emotional insights, and poetry brings my experience of the 2018 Puna eruption to a new, more spiritual level. Thank you for your talents. I hope many others sit down with ***Red Dreams, Volcano Visions*** for an amazing journey."

> — Harry Durgin,
> photographer,
> Puna resident

"Reading ***Red Dreams, Volcano Visions***, I soon found myself on the Big Island, caught up in a world of unpredictable dangers, infused with a paradoxical mood in which fear and alarm rubbed shoulders with awesome glory. Wow! I imagine enduring that 'stay or leave' tug-of-war that ensues when ties to home exert their pull, while fears of injury and death push hard from behind . . . when you consciously don't know what will happen next or how bad it will get before it's finally over. Surely living with an ongoing volcanic eruption going off in your backyard calls forth another set of contrasts too . . . the adrenaline-pumping hyperawareness of living moment to moment, and the enervating stress and fatigue that wear one to the bone . . . building up and breaking down as the dance of yin and yang create the ever-changing world, within and without."

— Katherine Shelley Orr,
author,
environmentalist

Red Dreams

Volcano Visions

Other Books by This Author

Footprints Wings Phantasms. Ka`a`awa, HI: Pacific Raven Press, 2018.

Shadow Dancing: $elling $urvival in China. Ka`a`awa, HI: Pacific Raven Press, 2017.

Zimbabwe Spin: Politics and Poetics. Ka`a`awa, HI: Pacific Raven Press, 2015.

*Love`s Seasons: Generations Genetics Myths*. Ka`a`awa, HI: Pacific Raven Press, 2014.

Timmy Turtle Teaches. Children`s book. Ka`a`awa, HI: Pacific Raven Press, 2012.

Frank Marshall Davis: The Fire and the Phoenix (A Critical Biography). Ka`a`awa, HI: Pacific Raven Press, 2012.

Tourmalines: Beyond the Ebony Portal. Ka`a`awa, HI: Pacific Raven Press, 2010.

*Pacific Raven: Hawai`i Poems*. Ka`a`awa, HI: Pacific Raven Press, 2009. (Winner of 2010 American Book Award from the Before Columbus Foundation.)

New and Collected Poems. Berkeley, CA: Ishmael Reed Publishing, 2003.

Oral Histories of African Americans. Interviews by Kathryn Waddell Takara. Center for Oral History. Social Science Research Institute. Honolulu, HI: University of Hawai`i at Mānoa, 1990.

Red Dreams
Volcano Visions

Kathryn Waddell Takara, PhD

Edited by Mera Moore

Pacific Raven Press

Ka`a`awa, Hawai`i

http://pacificravenpress.co

Pacific Raven Press, LLC
Ka`a`awa, Hawai`i 96730

ISBN: 978-0-9993039-4-8
ISBN (ebook): 978-0-9993039-6-2

Cover design and concept by Jonathan Zane

Fhotographs by Kathryn W. Takara

Book layout by Jonathan Zane, Eien Design
www.eiendesignstudio.com

Executive Editor: Mera Moore
Contributing Editor: Karla Brundage

This work is licensed under Pacific Raven Press, LLC.

Library of Congress Cataloging-in-Publication Data
Red Dreams, Volcano Visions
by Kathryn Waddell Takara, PhD
Catalogued as: Poetry, Philosophy, Environment, Hawaiian Mythology

Printed in the United States of America

Pacific Raven Press, LLC, is an independent publisher.
http://pacificravenpress.co/
pacificravenpress@yahoo.com

Dedication

To my ancestors, parents, children,
grandchildren, friends, and supporters.

To the energy and power of the
Hawaiian goddess of fire, *Pele*.

To posterity and growth
through pressure, release, and healing.

Table of Contents

List of Illustrations

All photos by Kathryn Waddell Takara

Acknowledgments

Alexandra Avery
Catherine Kalama Becker, PhD
Karla Brundage
Dane Dupont
Harry Durgin
Miles Jackson, PhD
Lilikalā Kame`eleihiwa, PhD
Joan Koff, PhD
Mera Moore, PhD
Katherine Shelley Orr
Harvey Takara
Imani Washington
Olivia York
Jonathan Zane

xxii

Foreword

By Liza Simon

Red Dreams, Volcano Visions by award-winning author Kathryn Waddell Takara presents this unfolding story with compassion, imbuing it with both local and universal resonance. This is an epic poem, which sets out to chronicle the 2018 eruption. It captures the voices of people in Puna coming together to share their ideas, feelings, thoughts, and opinions, their *mana`o*—local style—in protracted "talk story" sessions.

Through Takara's warm and loping lens, we see the residents rejecting the imposed label of "evacuees," holding fast to their respective identities, whether "indigenously rooted" or "homesteader rural" or "hippie renegade." Their differences are outweighed by what they share: love for the lands of Pele that they have tended side by side in peace.

Dedicated—for now—the lands are inextricable from who the residents are as a people. And so they stand in solidarity while yearning for a healing. Ordered by authorities to leave, they yearn to return—even if all they get is a temporary all-clear signal with a mandatory order to don gas masks, which prompts them to continue their vigil and hope for a miracle.

It goes without saying that Takara not only captures the pathos but does so with an ear for the constant local invocation of Pele. She portrays this ever so poetically as a "code-switching technique" to summon all things uniquely Hawaiian. Inherent in this cultural portrait is praise for the stewardship which enabled the first peoples of Hawai`i—the *kanaka maoli*—to ply intrepidly the vast Pacific and thrive in the extreme isolation of the isles they settled, wanting for nothing because their relationship of reciprocity with the Earth ebbed and flowed like the ocean waves that brought them here.

No stranger to themes of nature, Takara's previous books of poetry—eight in all—are deeply informed by an ecological consciousness. With ***Red Dreams, Volcano Visions,*** Takara establishes herself firmly within the emerging genre of eco-poetry which recognizes that our human existence arises out of nature, is dependent on nature, and cannot endure in isolation from nature because nature is a system of reciprocity and interdependence.

In May 2018, the first of many flaming fountains of lava erupted amidst a bucolic community in Puna, a coastal region of Kīlauea. Riveting as it was, it was hardly an unexpected turn of events. Found on the southeast side of Hawai`i Island, Kīlauea has been erupting and sending various configurations of molten rock down its slopes and out into the ocean for the last four decades. But the latest sequence of events went on and on and on—relentlessly so—accompanied by earthquakes, acid rain, and toxic explosions of volcanic gases.

Widely acknowledged as one of the world's most active volcanoes, Kīlauea suddenly took on many more superlatives. This new eruption was the most hazadous in Kīlauea's recorded history, burying over 700 homes and forcing the evacuation of thousands of residents. Teams of scientists arrived to investigate the drivers of such singular destruction and turned Kīlauea into the most studied volcanic mass of the 21st century. When news crews from everywhere converged on the scene, they produced stunning visuals that assured Kīlauea's fury would set a social media record for the most "hits" garnered by any natural disaster to date.

Those who call this earthen caldron of simmering magma their home were hardly immune to the awe felt by outsiders, but for them the latest eruption also ignited an unprecedented reckoning. They chose to live here knowing the risks of a volcanic disaster are so high that they will be denied property insurance. But the attainability of insurance policies was likely not what drew them to this place; rather it is the thrall of Pele herself, which makes the risks worthwhile. It is like being in a relationship where your heart eclipses the prospects of loss and pain—and your fondest hope is that it will do so forever.

Throughout ***Red Dreams, Volcano Visions,*** pieces of the Pele legend provide a shorthand re-affirmation of the reverence for nature that was eclipsed by the overthrow of the Hawaiian Kingdom in 1895. This includes the verses where *kūpuna* (elders) make not-so-veiled references to the carelessness and ignorance of Pele's ways. Takara picks up on how some elders lend credence to one prevailing view that a nearby geothermal plant's tapping of Kīlauea grounds for the production of energy contributed to instability of the land and the resulting fissures that were the spectacular hallmark of the 2018 eruption. She captures elders' metaphoric language comparing the company's industrial operations to the legendary precursor of Pele whose appetite for eating land with fire was never leavened with Pele's positive efforts of regeneration. Thus, without a hint of dogma, Takara infuses her poetry with the caginess of eco-poetic protest made palatable but powerful, because like political satire it works on an emotional level—woven into art.

Political protest may not have been the point of the ancestral versions of Pele legends, but the charm of legends is that they are fluid and expansive. Pele anthropomorphizes tribulations of love and hate so that they can erupt not only physically but psychically in language, shaping words that are then agents of change. In ***Red Dreams, Volcano Visions***, Pele's tribulations are not only about exploitation of natural resources but about the unjust treatment of people in an out-of-control capitalist system which accumulates wealth for a few by extracting sweat equity from the many. By enlisting

Pele to imply the ethical failings of all types of exploitation, this work of poetry inspires us to consider the value of cultivating a more balanced give-and-take across all relationships.

Native Hawaiian traditions of *hula* and chant tell us Pele is the ancient fire goddess. Haumea, aka Papahānaumoku, gave birth to the Hawaiian Islands. Haumea was the mother of Pele who was born in Tahiti and came to Ni`ihau via Borabora. Then from Ni`ihau she came down to Hawai`i Island. The wisdom of the traditions is woven into the mindset of those who inhabit the islands today.

They say that to live in the presence of Pele is to know her primordial powers of creation and destruction, to have faith that what she takes away she will also give back, to find spiritual solace in belonging to something greater than the self, something deliciously mysterious, something that beckons with infinitely new insights and possibilities.

But as weeks of Pele's latest tirade stretched into months, Pele's tenants were at last confronted with the reality that the paradoxical powers of this deity were genuinely beyond their ken and their control.

Her molten lava eventually hardened and many took it as a sign to harden their resolve to salvage what Pele gave them: if not their homes then at least some intangible bonds of the Puna community. But that turned into no easy task. When Pele finally went quiet, five months after she had roared to life, the media spotlight on Kīlauea had dimmed. Scientists had retreated to sift through big data. Meanwhile, back at ground zero, what was once an off-the-grid dream made manifest was now a hellscape of lava devastation dotted with makeshift shelters and a few stalwart structures that escaped incineration. Outside of the glare of the worldwide spotlight, the local story of people living with Pele continues.

It is a story of human pathos—and it applies not only to the folks of Kīlauea but to all of us who find ourselves at a crossroads fraught with our intentions and our inventions of unrestrained industrial growth and material consumption at odds with the inexorable cycles of nature. We may opt to ignore nature in all her terrifying mystery, but, when we do, we may find that we put ourselves and the future of our planet in peril.

Moving seamlessly from the political to the personal, Takara's epic poem indulges in lyrical praise for Kīlauea's lush verdant attractions—untouched by lava. But this is only a brief respite from the more disturbing passages that bear witness to the rampaging walls of fire that, by the standards of Pele worshippers, citizens, and world-class volcanologists alike, were truly terrifying to witness. It is worth noting that the author's impulse is neither to shrink from the terror nor to appropriate it as the personification of a human enemy. That was the habit of poets in the Western Romantic era whose individualistic depictions of a wonton wilderness gave rise to the colonialist notion that nature and its resources would be best served by human conquest—specifically their conquest. Clearly, ***Red Dreams, Volcano Visions*** signals a new and strident tact to the art of nature poetry, which has garnered the name eco-poetry.

The sub-text of today's eco-poetry, including ***Red Dreams, Volcano Visions,*** is climate change, the disorienting dilemma that for too long was understood as a problem of the physical sciences best addressed by policy and technology. But as harm of climate change brings us face to face with global habits of human activities that make us all both perpetrators and victims, we have come to know that this is a human problem: a problem which cannot be fixed without changes in our ethical and moral relationships within the natural world.

Poetry may initially strike us as a wan weapon in the face of such an enormous threat. But like the Pele legend in Takara's new work tells us, stories told in the unrestrained language of poetry have a way of digging under devastation, surmounting great barriers of flame, and outlasting emotional waves of grief and joy to restore us to a place where we can truly feel at home with all life. And that place is Earth, a place where our stories—and our passions for sharing our stories—keep us human.

Liza Simon-Tuiolosega is a local journalist and "choreopoet." She currently teaches and conducts research at the University of Hawai`i in the field of climate humanities.

Preface

Kathryn Waddell Takara

With ***Red Dreams, Volcano Visions***, I aim to present contemporary ecological and environment issues in the context of a volcanic eruption. My goal is to elevate readers' consciousness from a moral desert of conscience and caring to a level of moral awareness. I seek to transform the abuse of magnificent *Nature* to another level of respect for life, sustenance, and a healing of the Earth.

I want to provide compelling, intimate poetic impressions of the 2018 volcanic eruption at *Mauna Kea* on the *Big Island of Hawai`i*. I include vivid descriptions of the violent awakening of *Pele*, the fire goddess of *Halema`uma`u Crater* at the *Mauna Kea* volcano.

My poems explore Hawaiian mythology, disquieting red lava flows, and the daily community losses of land, homes, and livelihood. Some speculate that the destruction was caused by ignorance, irreverence for the sacred land and its power, and the greed of the developers who sold land on a high-risk rift zone.

I illuminate my readers about the *kanaka maoli*, the native people of *Hawai`i*, their spiritual traditions, history, continuing reverence for *Nature*, and the significance of the ancestral memories, legends, and myths on contemporary practices and lifestyles.

I accompany the eco-poems with my own startling photographs of the 2018 eruption. They communicate my firsthand experiences of the feel of the red heat, the sounds of the lava river, the intense changing colors, and crackling, burning foliage.

Via virtual technology, I also witnessed the eruptions, disruptions, and pain that transformed into community solidarity. I recognized the continuing transition of *Puna* district residents from indescribable loss by fire and lava to a process of healing through their heroic efforts, faith, and love of community.

My subtext is a commentary on the climate crisis and dire situation and conditions of our Earth. I observe the relationship between humanity and *Nature* and the unpredictable and predictable consequences of our abuse of our planet. Toward that end, my poetry includes philosophical and metaphysical questions of identity, conscience, and transformation.

I bear witness to neocolonial and colonial geologies and geographies of resistance and the psychological effects of loss and restoration in a social context of race, class, and culture. My message: we must get right with the earth.

The Magnitude of Endurance

Just before I left *Hawai`i* for California
to attend the MFA graduation of my
daughter, Karla, the *Big Island* volcano
known as *Kīlauea* erupted alarmingly.
Unpredictable fissures opened all across the
Lower East Rift Zone (*LERZ*).

She accompanied me back to *O`ahu*
and flew to *Hilo* to visit with her father
my first husband, who lives there.
They invited me to join them, and
grateful for their kindness I made plans.
Little did I know then how much I would
learn about the magnitude of endurance.

It was June 2018. A *Strawberry Moon*
beautifully illuminated the summer sky
so named by the Native American
Algonquin tribes to mark the season
to harvest delicious ripening wild berries.

Before dawn, I awoke to finish packing
and to perform a teaching commitment
at the *Kahalu`u* community Key Project.

At last arriving at the airport, I discovered
no license and no debit and credit cards—
checking in for my flight was impossible!

My second husband, who had driven me
an hour to the airport, considerately
volunteered to do the two-hour round-trip
to and from our home in *Ka`a`awa*.

Searching for the delicate silver card case
I'd bought a decade before on *Kaua`i* at a
Native American Powwow, he had no luck.
Instead, he found and brought to the airport
my passport, so at least I had a picture ID.
My dear husband kissed me goodbye and
left for home, a fourth hour on the road.

And I departed for *Hawai`i Island*, where
discoveries of pain and hardships by those
dispossessed by unrelenting flows of lava
awaited, where suffering multitudes would
teach me the magnitude of endurance.

Uncharted and Unknown

Issued a new boarding pass at no extra cost
I took off three hours later than intended
on the one-hour flight to the *Big Island*
where my daughter was patiently waiting.
Since May 3rd, the volcano had created
hundreds of small earthquakes throughout
Halema`uma`u Crater and *Puna* District.

The *Fissure 8* eruption had destroyed 500+
houses in the *Lower East Rift Zone (LERZ)*
displacing more than 1,000 people
who fled scarlet rivers of lava
slow *a`a* and fast *pohoehoe* flows
that scorched through *Leilani Estates*
and beyond down to *Kapoho*.

After a quick and uneventful flight, as the
plane landed, I saw the not-too-distant dark
ominous plume of smoke from the volcano.

My daughter Karla met me at the airport.
Needing four-wheel drive, we rented a jeep
then picked up her dad from the facility
where he was receiving physical therapy
and medical treatments for his ailing health.

Up the mountain we drove to inspect
the family property in Hawaiian Acres.
Modest house, small studio, fish pond
and the overgrown gardens filled with
huge, hearty trees, flowers, and fire ants.

The eruption smoke reached even here.
Up country, we could still smell the *vog*.
Yet life burst forth in solitude
mere miles from where the fire consumed
everything that lived, with or without eyes.

Trees were laden with bananas, papayas
guavas. From branches, orchids dangled
abundantly. On the ground, colorful
anthuriums and gingers grew luxuriously.
Vegetables untended lived in their chaos:
tomatoes here, cucumbers there, bits of
rosemary, thyme, and mint everywhere.

Red Dreams

Volcano Visions

Part I

Hawaiian Legends and Myths

The Approach

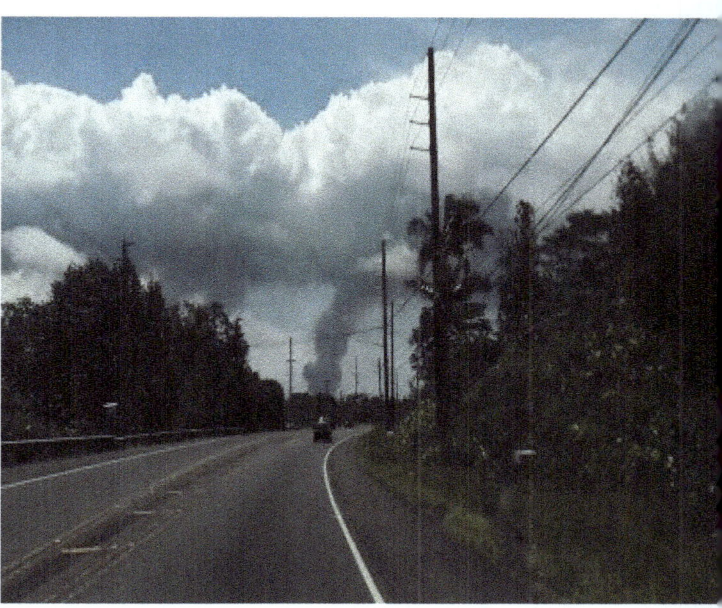

Visible and Invisible

On the instinctive, emotional edge
since May 3, 2018.
Disruptions plenty!

The earth cracks open.
Fissures erupt.
Surprise explosions multiply.
Lava channels form, rise, fall, flow.
With levees breached
no stopping her now
the viscous sizzling.

From *Fissure 8, Pele* belches
continuous, roaring red fountains.
Fluctuations romp in and out.
Lava and gases dance drunkenly.
Acid rain kills softly.
Trees are darkened
grass and flowers dried
all vegetation burned and buried.

Lava walls reach 30-to-50 feet in the air.
Hot spots change in patterns of eruptions.
From creeping *a`a* to fast-moving *pahoehoe*
the molten rock gains relentless momentum

blocking passages and leaving behind
scorched trees and telephone poles.
Wide swaths of green *Nature*
come tumbling down.
The smoky air causes respiratory ailments.
Electricity is disrupted for weeks then months.

The National Guard troops arrive:
set up roadblocks, barricade subdivisions
prohibit dangerous and uncertain areas
regulate vehicles and foot traffic
control access to entrances and exits
and are on the lookout for thieves and looters.

Before goddess *Pele* arrived on *Hawai`i Island*

Kīlauea was controlled by *`Ai Lā`au*
a frightening god who decimated
with burning lava yet created land.
There, enduring rain made streams and rivers
and people cultivated fields and built homes.

When *Pele* came, *`Ai Lā`au* disappeared.
Some *kanaka maoli* question:
Has *`Ai Lā`au* returned?

Huna Moon

Answers unknown.

Secret purification
underneath a *huna* moon
that hides its horns and grows round.

House of silver light
shimmers on the `*ōhi`a lehua* trees
in the legendary domains.

The *Farmers' Almanac* recalls
a time of freedom in the cycles
of the ancient lunar goddess *Mahina.*

It instructs when to plant seeds
how to transplant and nurture them
with precious water and moonbeams.

Yet it cannot predict eruptions.

Goddess *Pele*

There's trouble in so-called paradise
on *Hawai`i,* the *Big Island*
56,000 feet above the ocean floor
at *Halema`uma`u Crater*
legendary abode of *Pele*, the fire goddess.

Her awakening, fiery red and passionate
surprises volcanologists, geologists, tourists.
The ecosystems are shaken
catching communities and *Nature* off guard.

Pele births alerts, eruptions, explosions.
Then 24 steaming fissures appear
change daily, crack the earth
exhale malodorous sulfur
destroy idyllic dreams of peaceful living
of swimming in seductive turquoise waters.

Pele is the powerful goddess of fire
familiar in *Puna* and beyond.

Nemesis of her compassionate sister
loyal and loving *Hi`iakaikapoliopele*

Pele coughs up her retaliatory magic
devouring forests and all organic life
destroying the homes of *kanaka maoli*
and non-Hawaiian individualists alike.

Paradoxically, as *Pele* exhales destruction
her violent releases makes new land
with the fountaining magnitudes of lava!

Deep under the Earth's crust, *Pele* inhales
mixing her mysterious, furious magma
stirring up the alchemy of re-creation.

The Awakening

Creator and destroyer, invisible and visible
explosive, luminous, magenta
temptress goddess in outbursts of passion
Pele appears suddenly in late spring 2018
blasting up fissures of fire and sulfur.

She devastates residents' paradisiacal dreams
razes the calm aqua bays
and the healing *Ahalanui Warm Ponds*.

Pele's awakening, rusty red
flamboyant and passionate
dances in rhythmic fountains
shakes the ecosystems
destroys all in her path
(*Nature*, communities, property)
unleashes more growing, moving outbreaks.

Pele's dynamic, cardinal-red power
rises stunningly
exploding from the widening crater
her manifesto to all
from angry Mother Earth.

A magnitude of lava egresses
previously unmatched
pushes outward—on the increase!

Pele's extravagant eruption
portends destruction, pain, loss
foreshadows resurrection
creates transformation
builds new land
for future expansion
and new settlements, or not.

Pele and *Fissure 8*

It's a spectacular show, lava fireworks
ominous, eerie, fiery-painted skies.

There are variable, color-filled clouds
corals, magentas, rubies
irregular shades of gray and black.

Surprising impermanent weather
patterns appear
while molten rock gushes torrential
reveals the heartbeat of *Fissure 8*.

Kanaka maoli understand
the powerful process.

Let go of illusions of control.
Allow for the robust untamed cycle
of evolution.
Recognize the signs.

It's still too smoky
to fathom the future
in an unpredictable present.

Fissures from on High

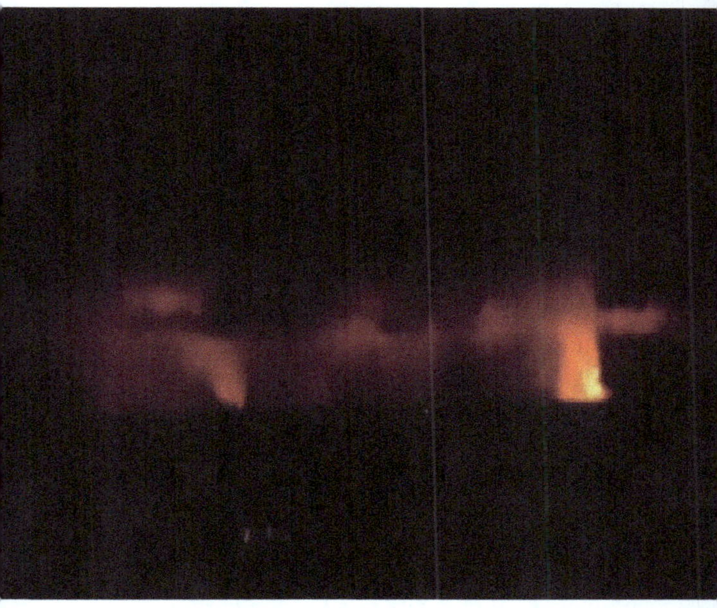

Listen to Lessons Learned

Kūpuna, ancestors, spirits
use stories and fables
wisdom, symbols, signs
speak magnetic words.

Hear the crystalline voices of the free wind.
Smell the fresh morning.
In beautiful *Hawai`i nei*
are the sounds of neighbors
children`s varied voices
humming, singing, murmuring, teaching
playing familiar games.

Words free and powerful cure with laughter
or can wound, threaten, hurt.
Hazy conditions sully the day, but . . .
the *Cheshire Cat* smiles
silently blowing smoke rings.
An elusive Buddha sits in a hidden garden.

Blue sulfur from nearby *Halema`uma`u*
drifts over land and sea like toxic incense.
What is too much light?

The Radiant Sisters

Pele, powerful fire goddess
calm, then violent and unpredictable
is jealous and angry, a trickster.

Hi`iaka
whose full name is *Hi`iakaikapoliopele*
the beautiful "sunrise goddess"
dwells in delicate fragrance
near gingers, white *naupaka*, and *tiare*
dances under the *Mahealani* moon.

Hi`iaka smiles in the season of harvests
in the islands of love and sweetness.

Goddess of new life
and rejuvenation of the earth
with the astonishing growth
of *kupukupu, pala`ā*, and *palapalai ferns*
immediately after a lava flow
is kind and loving, graceful and gentle.

As *Pele* exhales hot destruction
eating the forest and making new land
Hi`iaka luminously observes.

Hi`iakaikapoliopele

Hi`iaka, the glorious dancer of *hula*
was summoned by her fiery sister, *Pele*
who longed to reunite with *Lohi`au*
whom she loved, a young chief and singer
from the *mokihana* mountains of *Kaua`i*.

Lohi`au did not know that *Pele* was a goddess
and neither sister knew
that he would later want to flee *Pele`s* power.

Pele asked *Hi`iaka* to bring *Lohi`au* to her
within 40 days and without embracing him.
Hi`iaka agreed, and with her companion
the half-goddess *Wahine `Oma`o*
embarked on her appointed mission.

Trade winds chanted magical tunes of romance
to *Pele*, who rested in her bubbling lava pits
at the volcano Kīl*auea*, high above *Hilo*
land of the red *`ōhi`a lehua* blossoms
and slept, exulting in her deep dragon dream.

Leaving behind the guardian winds of *Puna*
Hi`iaka traveled on kite-flying currents
up the chain of the Hawaiian islands
with three spiritual gifts as tools
super strength, a lightning skirt
and a critical eye with supernatural knowledge.

As *Hi`iaka* traveled, the mists drifted low.
The caves echoed the mocking winds
over mountain precipices, warning of danger
yet the faithful ocean currents remained calm.

She knew she held *mana*
power protecting her journey
from hidden mold-green demons and goblins.

When *Hi`iaka* arrived in *Kaua`i*
she found that *Lohi`au* had died
from longing for Pele.

Through chanting and prayer
Hi`iaka revived and returned him
but missed the deadline of 40 days.

Pele had promised to protect
the beloved forests of *Hi`iaka* in *Puna*
but feeling betrayed, impatient, angry
and unfaithful to her word
she destroyed the forests
with her unrelenting dance
of immediate gratification of vengeance.

When *Hi`iaka* returned
and saw *Pele*'s destruction
she took her revenge, embracing *Lohi`au*.
Once again, *Pele*'s anger flared
spewing lava across the island
and turning *Lohi`au* to stone.

Can a goddess learn lessons or not?

Travels of *Hi`iaka*

Hi`iaka, goddess-sister of *Pele*
befriended the divine guardians
of plants and forests.

Hi`iaka was sent by *Pele*
on a quest to find *Lohi`au*, *Pele*'s paramour.
She crossed the channels between islands
passed though forests over mountains
the air full of fire vents, *vog*
cold rains and biting winds.

She met monsters of supernatural powers
who governed all harmful creatures
residing from the mountain to the sea
who tangled trees and branches to obstruct
the safe passage of unsuspecting intruders.

Exhausted from fighting monstrous obstacles
Hi`iaka was wounded, weary, nearly dead
her magic skirt tattered—but still victorious.

When she finally rested in the forest shadows
she saw her enemies slain all around her.
Green guardians protected her royal journey.

Fire, *Pele*, and *`Ai Lā`au*

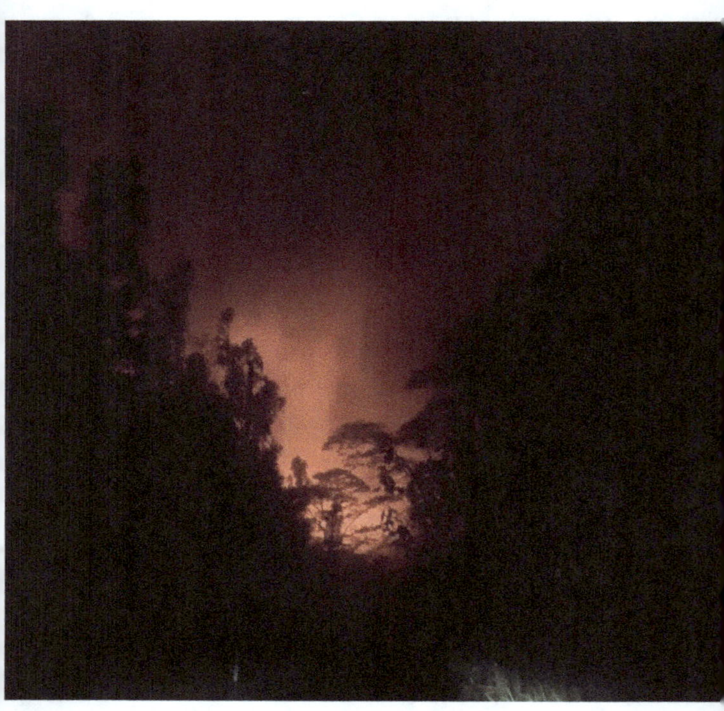

Remembering `Ai Lā`au

Myths, legends, oral histories affirm
`Ai Lā`au occupied *Halema`uma`u*
before *Pele*'s coming.

He was formerly in possession of
an ancient area of *Kīlauea* called *Kīlauea-iki*
a small sunken pit
the first in a line of the great path of fire
on the rift to the seacoast ten miles away.

Known and respected by the Hawaiian people
`Ai Lā`au was named the Forest Eater
a fire-god who devoured organic life.
He was feared for his power.
His flame arose from the belly of the pit.

Legend says he abandoned the small place
moved to the great crater
where he lived for eras
until *Pele* came seeking a permanent home.
The fatherly fire god gave to her his throne
of fire and power.

Kūpuna speculate that perhaps he has returned
at *Fissure 8*
fueling the lava flow
increasing the eruption
exacting retribution
for increasing abuse
disrespect of the `*āina*.

`*Ai Lā`au* and *Pele* disrupted land and lives
with vindictive power: passion, fire, poisons.

`Ai Lā`au

Did the legendary *`Ai Lā`au* return?
The *kūpuna* silently evoke the question.

The volcanic cone named *Ahu `Ai Lā`au*
stands near *Fissure 8*
defies ongoing whirlwinds
fire twisters, smoky tornados
reds, oranges, magentas, yellows changeable.

Daily alerts increase.
New flows surprise.
Enormous amounts of deadly emissions
dangerous levels of SO2.
Non-stop lava from *Fissure 8*
builds new *pu`u*, volcanic cones
along her fire-strewn path.

Is *`Ai Lā`au* really with *Pele*
together wreaking wrath
in relatively new settlements, cracking more
highways, roads, parking lots, gardens, homes
even in *Hawai`i Volcanoes National Park*?
No answer, no science, no comment.
A`a and *pohoehoe* lava continue to flow
in record-breaking amounts of cubic lava.

The flow braids and hardens in code
another language out of time.
Science and mythology meld
in the scarlet heat.

Lava cooled exposes surreal forms
tubes, rainbow colors, iridescent shapes.
It inspires artistic expressions
reminds of long-ago stories
myths and metaphors of life
true or not true
important or not.

Answers unknown.

Pele and `*Ai Lā`au*

The question remains:
who and what is responsible
for the ring of fire and recent rift zones
the unprecedented eruption
of record-breaking quantities of lava?

Is `*Ai Lā`au* indeed a co-conspirator with *Pele*?
Observe how the flow size spreads
magnifies, increases.
Who or what is in control? Not humans.

Every witness learns more about volcanoes.
Knowledge grows like power.
Understanding comes with awe
the multiple lessons of letting go
of drinking and swallowing tears, fears, regrets.

In face of an eruption, egos must surrender
or be forced to submit to loss and destruction
to allow for perennial change.
Humans are humbled
powerlessness, surrender.
Prominence is swallowed
by a powerful, dominant, invisible might.

Part II

Danger and Alerts

Lower East Rift Zone (LERZ)

Peaceful beauty, remote rural settings
and forested lands are destroyed
in the *Lower East Rift Zone (LERZ)*.

Gone:
Leilani Estates, Green Mountain, Four Corners
and crucial electric, telephone, and cable lines.
Gone:
Ahalanui Warm Ponds, Kapoho Tide Pools
and the famous surf spots *Bowls and Shacks*.
Gone:
Kapoho Village, Beach Lots, Malulani Circle
and newer communities gated in recent times.

Highways are blocked and roads split
making travel and escape difficult.
Papaya Farms Road and *Noni Farms Road*
remain untouched, and *Pohoiki* still stands.
Ahalanui Beach Park is still spared for now.

Nothing and no one can resist
the monster lava flow
that destroys then builds more land.

Cascading photos and memories
are witness to the transformation.
In the fire-river rapids that ebb and flow
people see dancing skeletons and ghosts.
Images of *Pele* rising from the lava
inspire artistic expressions
by those with creative imaginations.

Armies of animals wander
panicked, lost, forsaken
the flow threatening from all sides.
Where can they run to survive?

Multiple crimson veins of lava
arrive at the coast and stall.
Smoking danger looms at the ocean entry.
The lava builds, resurges, slowly approaches
Pohoiki, the boat ramp, the *Red House*.

People pray with the residents
that the eruption stop before destruction
of the precious local fishing spots
and recreation areas mainly for locals
threatening the loss of livelihood.
When will *Pele* stop? Where are you?

Loss of Dreams

Listen.
Hear the viscous crackling
rumbling vibrations.
Feel the earth shake loudly
move to cracking protest.
Noise crescendos and decreases hourly
through the days, weeks, months
of continuing evacuations
and uncertainty.

Sadness scratches the air.
Children cry, dogs bark, skittish cats hide.
Grownups wail quietly, try to protect the
children with illusions of safety
experience the corrosive loss
of one and many dreams.

Wake up! Stay woke!
Recognize the constant rumbling voice
of *Pele*'s process.

Visions Tattoo My Mind

Watch.
Kīlauea crater erupts
on May 3, 2018, after a 6.9 earthquake
Continual aftershocks rock the *Puna* district.

In just a few days
24 fissures violently open
spout rocks, fire, steam, and gases
block passages and access to homes
mirroring the unceasing orgasms
of Earth`s inner movements.

Rolling lava and polluted air
force the rapid evacuation
of several thousands of people
dream homes, various structures
agricultural lands
farm animals, and pets
near and around
the unknown pathway of the lava
which builds and spreads
for over four months!
This new incandescent eruption
is awesome and terrifying.

Tall, alarming fiery fountains
of destruction and paradoxical growth
create unforgettable visions
excite the imagination.
There are lava rivers, rapids, burgs.
Boats become fire monsters, stalking the land.

Micro weather systems
with lightning, thunder
occasional fire tornados
appear and disappear
like incomprehensible symbols
localized in pockets of towns
established subdivisions
idyllic vacation rentals.

Decimated dreams of a good life
in a chosen idyllic place
melt in the unrelenting lava.

The feeling of loss is tattooed on my mind.

Danger Electric

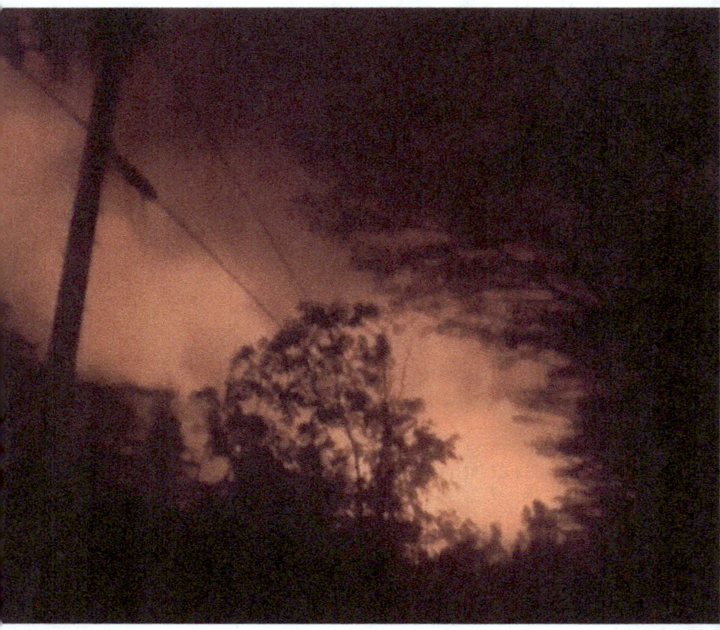

Beauty and Terror

Dawn has come and gone, returns again
after the door of night slowly opens
to the light of day.

Fissure 8 broadens
dominates, spreads, threatens
homes and structures, gardens and forests
lakes and tide pools.

The eruption unleashes cascading rapids of fire
lava balls, lava boats, floating debris.

The wide river of provocative lava rages
tramples across *Leilani Estates*
then cascading east toward *Pohoiki*
down to the oceanfront at *Kapoho*
and into the open ocean south of *Hilo*
following indifferent paths of least resistance.

Rough revelations: beauty and bareness
balance and imbalance
replicating vibrant red visions
maps of bloodstreams, veins, organic systems.

The clinging, cloying crimson fire
leaves acrid smells of burning vegetation
structures, animals, sea life.

Producing thick, unfamiliar terror
unpleasant odors hang in the windless air
affronting the breath, polluting the atmosphere
unfamiliar yet recognizable
measurable and immeasurable
smells, temperatures, emotions.

The Conditions

Smoke, sulfur, *vog*, and ash
permeate the otherwise usual pristine air.
Breathing and lung issues soar
skin and eye irritations too.
Atmosphere unpredictable and dangerous
levels too high in sulfur, SO2.

Unknown invisible poisons
blanket the environment in *Puna*
from *Kapoho Village* to *Leilani Estates*
from *Pāhoa* to *Hawaiian Acres*
from *Pahala* to *Ka`u* and beyond
around to *South Point* and up to *Kona.*
Area warnings abound, multiply.

Dangerous winds transport
the miniscule, translucent
volcanic glass threads
that float like fine needles, embed like mites
penetrate the eyes, skin, lungs
without protective cloths or gas masks.

Sudden rains
and fluctuating temperatures transform
thick atmosphere of volcanic particles
into unforgettable olivine crystals.

One day
green jewels of olivine
tumble magically to Earth
from the smoke-filled dome.
Tephra falls like black feathers
of swirling snow
the size of quarters
blocks the drains and gutters.
Changing conditions prevail
variable, alluring, awe-inspiring.

Visions of Smoke and Masks

Respiratory and health issues proliferate
in extreme conditions of danger
both visible and invisible.

Shades of white, gray, black
intense reds, oranges, yellows
contrast vibrant island blues and greens.

Colors flare at sunrise, sunset
variations closer or farther
from the crater explosions.

Camouflaged hazards appear
sulfur vents, collapses of lava
methane cracks and tubes.

Ash, dust, particulate
tiny fractions of gas and glass
randomly fall like transparent tears.

Pele's hair burns dangerously
her powerful odors offensive to life.
Masks are donned with unpredictable winds.

Barely believable, the need for masks
worn by some for weeks on end.
The residents of the *LERZ* look like aliens!

People obtain scientific instruments
to measure/monitor air quality
for toxic smoke that can carry carcinogens.

Hazardous Air

Wizard winds change with fiery flare-ups
along channelized edges
blaze around the summit
blare across the valleys and communities
push through trees and forests.

Along channelized edges
new lava breakouts stun.
Impressive whirlpools of millennia magma
overrun logic.

Hazardous conditions invade then retreat.

Ephemeral magenta whirlwinds
sting the skin with volcanic ash
blanket, smother, and cover everything
on the trail of transformation.

Contaminated air is a threat
to all surrounding organic life.

Payback of *Pele*

Thick veil of *vog* invades the island, spreads
while the volcano rages fiery, alchemical loss.

Volcanologists with innovative instruments
walk around taking *USGS* measurements
monitor phases and changes of the fissures
use high-tech cameras, videos, other devices
to study the eruption's thermal tilt
intrusive drones providing incredible vistas.

Sometimes, mechanical eyes
see beyond the emotional panorama.

During the eruption, summer surf on the rise
hurricanes Hector, Lane, Olivia
slowly line up in succession
to invade and ruin all in their paths.
They conjure more anxiety
fear of loss of control, imbalance
portend more improbable disasters
unsuspecting calamities.

People whisper *Pele* and `*Ai Lā`au*
have returned to flaming power
to mitigate selfish appropriation
of Hawaiian lands
and cultural practices
disregarded and disrespected
by outsiders and settlers.

Some say the eruption is to rectify
the lack of reverence for Mother Earth
the exploitation of *Nature*
the abuse of the `*āina*, the *kai*, other beings
a payback for the ignorance of history
the absent respect and valuation
of the knowledge and wisdom
from the indigenous *kanaka maoli*.

All strive to balance the see-saw:
hope versus fear of more destruction.

Too Close in *Nanawale*

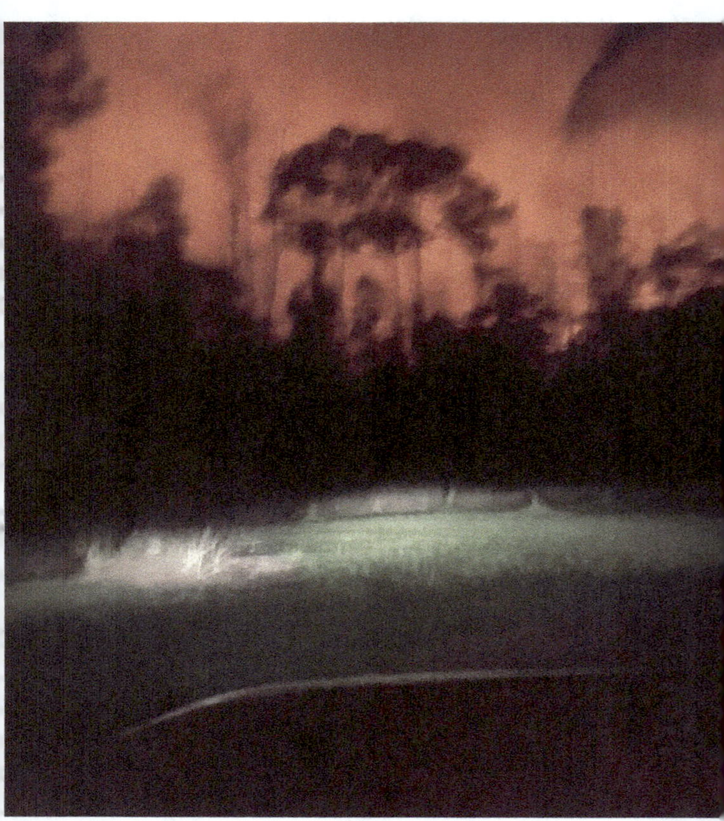

Relentless Flow

The mighty flow astounds all:
frightened residents who inhabit horror
loved ones far from them who long to help
observing empaths around the world.
Throngs follow the *Hawai`i* eruption.

With technologies, experts and residents
witness Earth's raw primal processes.
Helicopters, planes, boats, the internet
even the space station's global updates
intimately and objectively record the news.

The relentless 2018 eruption
stuns to fear and flight
tumbling, rumbling, cracking
beyond control and imagination.

The flow challenges the adventurers admirable
the settlers courageous
the many living off the grid
side by side with the risk takers
even some ex-cons and escapees.
The fiery fountains
the ever-expanding rivers of molten lava
build and collapse unpredictably.

The changing, shifting, awe-inspiring crater
produces a sour taste
of helpless emotions in a barren landscape.
The mostly unapproachable scene
feels like a soulless moon showcase.
A natural disaster flows toward all
in its soon-to-be barren path.

Beautiful *Volcano Village* and the *LERZ*
are daily tormented
by hundreds of earthquakes
for months of tremble.
Communities jolted
undulate under pressures
from deep within Earth`s crust.
Unstable ground and unsafe air
compel people to stay in place
close to where they eat and sleep.
Elemental expressions continue to amaze.

Earth, seasons, tides, eruptions
Mother Nature, the great teacher
unveil and expose our fears
and faith in the miracle of transformation.

Evacuations

A channelized lava river
two-and-a-half miles wide, eight miles long
pulses variably
like intricate veins, arteries, glands.

The molten fire hurtles along
at 15 mph, both less and more.
The lava heartlessly destroys all life
any obstacles in its path
structures, `*ōhana* compounds
elegant homes, vacation rentals
unlicensed and licensed.

The searing flow burns indiscriminately
wild and untamable animals, forests
food plots, farms
flower gardens, tide pools
vacation rentals, bed and breakfasts
Airbnb rooms and tiny houses, many illegal.

All can disappear or not
in a morning, overnight, in a breath
with little or no warning
even the landmark *Blue House*.

The people evacuate or remain
take red chances when they imagine
success or vulnerability.

Whenever Civil Defense arrives
morning, noon, afternoon
and even deep into the night
residents are caught unprotected
in the whimsical twists and turns
of *Pele*'s rampage
with only minutes available to escape.

Some people in frantic mode
stay in their homes prepared to flee at an
emergency warning.
They shelter wherever
and with whomever they can not ready to
accept personal destruction
hopeful that homes, belongings will be spared.

They witness beauty and fear, fire and water.
The tensions of opposite forces
clash like rivals.
Residents offer prayers
for safety and compassionate peace.

Science

The trees, telephone poles, houses, farms
food supplies are buried
all in the path of a relentless vermillion flow
down the mountain culverts and valleys
toward the azure ocean.

Earthquake patterns
appear and disappear.
Frequency and intensity
rise and fall like breath.
At times, 600-to-1,000 quake-shakes per day
almost unbelievable.

For five weeks daily
at least one quake over 5.0 magnitude occurs
finally slowing in August to one quake every
30-to-50 hour intervals.

All day and night
endless-seeming explosions from inside
Halema`uma`u Crater
rock *Volcano Village*.
The walls collapse.
The *Jaggar Museum*
and damaged trails are forced to close.

People and pets adjust.
Fires from snaking lava
imprint tastes of acid on tongues and in throats.

Efforts of animal-loving volunteers
continue for months.
They rescue mostly by helicopter
the trapped or abandoned pets
and surviving farm animals
deliver them to shelters, vets
foster families and new homes
help them to heal
from the trauma of abandonment
and near death.

Science, technology, and heartfelt compassion
make saving lives possible.

Danger

Laze, haze, maze, shaking terrain
carry smells of danger and death.

The variable winds, visible and invisible
depend upon the conditions and currents
the temperature, the topography.

Day and night, embedded in rain and *tephra*
toxic gases, steamy explosions
ash clouds, glass particles, *Pele*'s hot hair
are mostly blown to *Pahala* and beyond.

Few daily reports from or about the wild
mostly unpopulated district of *Ka`u*
south of *Hawai`i Volcanoes National Park*
are known.

Danger threatens the land and the people.

Part III

Fire

Lava, Lava, Lava!

August. Another week passes
in the supposed "paradise" called *Hawai`i*.
60-foot cliffs of lava
pause, tower above communities
threaten to cover all, temperaments on edge.

Lava continues to the tumble
blazing a path
into the previously predictable
peaceful sea instantly destroying
devouring beach homes, animals
pets, property, and open land
roiling the blue water
killing and boiling sea life
magenta fish, eels, blue fish, octopus
yellow fish, porpoises, silver fish, sea turtles.
Ahalanui Warm Ponds eaten by *a`a*
miles overflowed by *pahoehoe*.

Why is the Geothermal Plant still standing?

A new small island is observed
born out of the sea and thick, hot new lava.
The ocean swirls red all around the coast
soon after to be eaten by the growing channels.

An underwater lava tube
created by the powerful flow
opens and closes in hours.

Up the hill, shattering the cosmos
electrical storms irradiate energy.
Auras stain the sky orange, rose, purple, gray.
Unpredictable mini-climates
create nine inches of rain
hammering *Pāhoa* in one day.

Meanwhile, ten miles away, gentle breezes
blow under the sunny haze.
Miracle blue micro-atmospheres
manifest in nearby *Hilo,* and beyond.

Pāhoa and *Nanawale*

Volcano fires illuminate the *Pāhoa* clouds.
Acres of sky glow eerily
astound the night watchers.
Awesome, vivid colors
change hourly
divine yellows
brilliant oranges
dancing reds
romantic pinks
shouting vermilions.

One evening, I eat dinner in *Pāhoa*
with friends. We take pictures
alongside the crowds, all awestruck
by the glorious multicolored evening sky.

In my mind
I return regularly, at least twice daily
take virtual mind trips to *Pāhoa*
and to nearby *Nanawale*.

Nanawale, home of friends
is perched behind *Lava Tree Park*.

Fissure 8 roars
just behind their threatened community *hui*.
Residents wearing gas masks
witness the menacing ruby skies.

Clouds hover
sometimes angelic
sometimes satanic
appear predictably
over the eruption site
cover half the sky
on each otherwise dark night.

Alerts

"*Puna* Strong! Stay Classy!" *Ikaika*'s mantra
to surpass displacement, homelessness, loss.
Upbeat, he leads an online community.

Despite beeps, wails, sirens, buzzers, bullhorns
he posts updates hourly
and sets aside time for family care
plus his own meals, exercise, and imagination.

The Hub offers shelter, some comfort
a space and resource
for scientists, organizers, residents
to give, receive, and understand
the scope of the eruption
the significance of all alerts
to appreciate and value
intersections/interconnections/technology
and the abundant *aloha* of alert volunteers.

Puna Strong

Fissure 8 persists in powerful dominance
expresses beauty of human powerlessness
inspires astonishment, terror, trepidation
at the limitless lava and stunning surges.

Fissure 8 pumps, belches, shakes
angrily throwing out, throwing down
molten lava, pungent smoke
sizzling spatter, choking searing steam.

A *voggy* pattern of flow develops
from the crater and down the rift zone
changes possible moment to moment
pulses measurable and immeasurable.

Despite loss and mourning
fearful amazement and anticipation
displaced residents observe "*Puna* Strong!"
and daily good reminders to "Stay Classy!"

Puna remains a healing place
witness to transformative transference
experiencing preeminent moments
of humbling, awe-inspiring danger and despair.

Are Structures Safe?

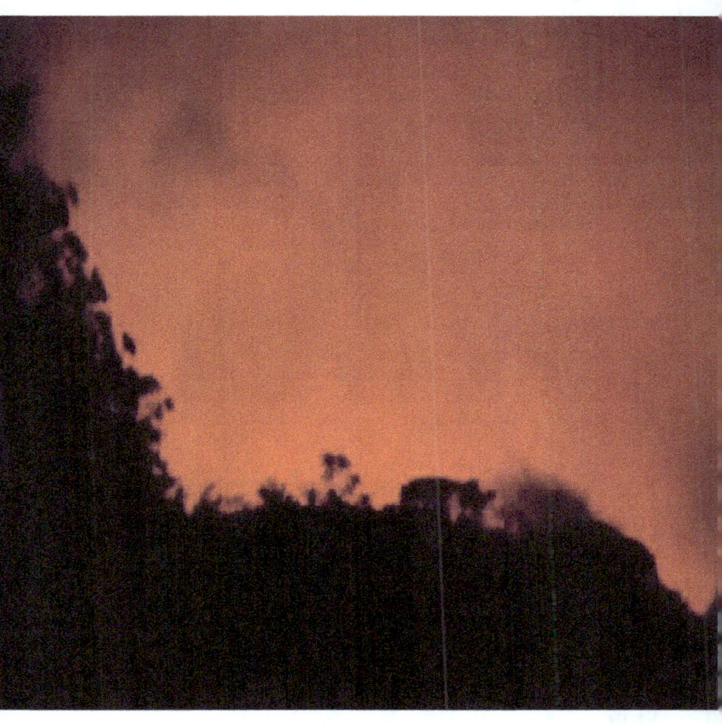

***Puna* Lament**

Too much eruption to fathom
earthquakes to digest, to accept.
Locals lament upended lifestyles
their ruined familiar daily routines.
Lost in uncertainty like collective dementia
lives grow rough when *Pele* comes around.

Fissure 8 dances abundantly
inspires effusive wonderment
while *Pele* destroys
Kapoho and *Vacationland*
parts of *Leilani Estates*.
Is confusion a high state of mind
opening to new possibilities?

People lament lost homes and pets
structures and subdivisions
livelihoods, farms, and jungles.

Lost is *Ahalanui Beach Park*
its treasured recreation areas
for fishing, snorkeling, swimming, surfing.
Gone is *Kua O Ka Lā* Charter School.

The future is unknown, uneasy.

Will the *Jaggar Museum*
and the popular trails and excursions
in *Hawai`i Volcanoes National Park*
be restored?

Will the famed *Volcano House*
and the gift store featuring local art
survive the closures and loss of tourists?

All lament the burned farms
flowers, fruits, and fauna
down and around the *LERZ*.

We rejoice at the possibility
of the coming end with restoration
that accompanies any disaster with gratitude.

At the Ocean Entry

Underwater lava explosions
surprise and astound
the tour boat pilots
threaten the unsuspecting, adventure-thirsty
tourists and guides
who somehow believed
in safe zones
measured in meters and feet
ironic situation in front of a powerful
eruption with no end in sight.

Imminent lava outbursts
throw out danger
fire rocks as large as pianos
hurled up and out beyond the coast.

Stunning erasure
of timeless predictable blue waters
turned boiling black
at the ocean entry.

Surfers, fishermen, beachgoers
bemoan and grieve the destruction
of favorite secret swimming and surf spots
Bowls, Secrets, all gone in a day.

Daily, we witness
the dangerous ocean entry
with lava and laze two miles wide.

Alerts. Will they never stop?
vol-canados, vol-collapses
new words arise to fit the conditions
lava boats
lava bergs
lava bombs
lava nados
a dark ring fire tornado
arises like smoke from the pipe
of the puffing *Cheshire Cat*.

When is the eruption slowing down?
A huge unknown hangs in each breath.

High and Deep

Hard to dream up the measurements.
Look, listen, see fiery images
unbearable inescapable unimaginable yet real.

The hot river channels are 40-to-70 feet deep
lava ponds ready to overflow into new territory
once deemed safe.
Moving lava walls
towering 50 feet high and more.

Fortunately, the new lava banks stand strong
discourage and forbid crumbling access
contain the lethal river.

Cameras capture ghosts of *Pele*
bouncing along in the flow
laughing, tossing hearts of splatter.

Fire dancing with the tremors and earthquakes
in the middle of the unexpected visions
the passionate feminine
untouchable, indestructible.

What makes an illusion verifiable?
What is true?

Pohoiki

Pohoiki and various homes, farms, structures
remain in imminent danger
under red warnings.

The lava horse continues to trot, gallop, race
past *Campbell Pond* with families of sea turtles
past *Bowls* and other bays
threatening the pier and local fishing holes.

Some lament the imminent loss
of historical *Pohoiki*.
Others visualize the end of the eruption
a new future
with sparkling air and water
a return to peace and calm.

The past has gone and not.
Never forgotten.

Patterns of Creation

Rolling boulders, lava boats, debris
race down towards the sea
in perched channels
levels variable, higher and lower
lava flow the constant
moving south
with increasing red and black volume
various arrivals
of voluminous vermillion
streams of scorching lava
tumbling into the ocean below
building new cliffs.

Burning Trees

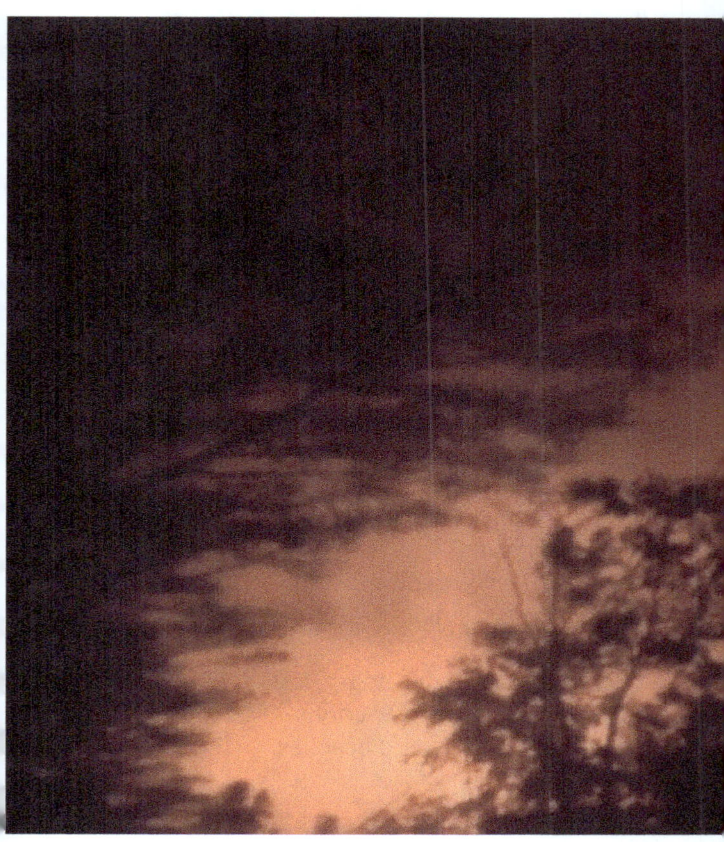

Last Stand

Where lava meets ocean
laze, winds, and waves
mix and whirl like *Pele*'s hair.
In a matter of days
the lava entry expands
one-to-two miles wide or more.

Huge plumes of fire
angry explosions
burst from the caldron
thrown 100 feet into the air
creating poisonous clouds.

The pungent smells of burning *Nature*
sear the air and lungs.

So much torrential lava
traps and kills the sea life
flows now more south
then more north
produces unforgettable angry emissions
watery eyes, chest constrictions
new land and black sand beaches.

Nightly, tall thick clouds
of incandescent colors
astound the mesmerized gazers.

Ocean entries spread
wrap around the bays and coastline.

People pray.
Pohoiki still stands
but for how long?
Will there be more destruction, or not?

Lava Boat Tours

Channels crack and spill over, split open
create new paths and dangerous flows
follow valleys of least resistance
to the crackling ocean entries.

Sunrise lava explosions surprise
a tour boat pilot and his clients.
Lava rocks crash on the passengers
some injured, boat severely damaged.

Outbreaks continue under the water
barely detectable
constant changes in the flow unstoppable.
What is deemed safe is also unpredictable.

Emitting crazy surges of liquid heat
waves and tides ebb and flow.
Violent threads of searing lava
appear and disappear in the water.

The fire dragon moves on
relentlessly to the sea at variable speeds
both slow and fast.

Warning: keep a safe distance!

Visuals and Visions

Look! Tangible changes shape-shift.
Quake numbers, lava out-pour rates change.
Fissure 8 roars, spits menacing crimson fire.
A trickster dragon pops a sketch then vanishes.

As flashes of clouds morph in the skies
colors transform into flying moments.
In sunlight, saffron sulfur splashes the sky
with spicy oranges, ruby reds, bloody yellows.

Sapphire swimming holes dry up
and emerald vegetation turns brown.
Yet sing a new music, Hallelujah!
Rainbow colors dance in drying lava crusts!

But translucent poisonous gases linger
measurable, immeasurable, visible, invisible.
Thunderous showers camouflage acid rain
killing the lungs of *Nature*, quickly and slowly.

Mystical transformations elude my instincts.
Is the eruption slowing down?

Visions and hopes fly moment to moment.
No comment. No comment.

Patience and Perseverance

Some output reports confuse the community.

Wait! Is *Fissure 22* coming alive again?
Is another fissure reopening?
Does the data portend a new eruption?

Patiently, residents hold a collective breath
experience re-births, external and internal.
Quizzical attitudes challenge the norms.

Questioning status, children ask:
"Why can't we go home?"
They reject separation/abandonment/death.

Valuing legacy, adults ask:
"What is valuable, ethical, moral?"
"Who and what can we trust?"
"Is anything regular and reliable?"

The eruption continues. People pray
for containment, endings, new beginnings.

Answers are vague and abstract.
Compassion rescues vulnerability.
Maybe hope arises or not.
In patience lies wisdom.
Is blind acceptance wise?

Foot-by-foot, from mountains to the sea
lava continually coughs forward, threatens
the forest and black sand beach of *Pohoiki*
but both receive a reprieve, along with
the 200-year-old *Red House* and boat ramp.

Menacing ocean temperatures
heat up fast at the lava entry.
The flow, 50-feet tall
overruns the shoreline and sea life
creating tall crumbling cliffs by the small bays.
For yet another day,
family homes still stand.
For how many hours, minutes, seconds more?

No one knows.
No one wisely dares to guess, predict.
In a place
where time is irrelevant
timing is everything.

Part IV

The Community Hub

The Hub Serves

The community continues to grow at the Hub
Pu`u Honua `O Puna
upgrading with soulful guides
daily building, cleaning
providing services and supplies
to the needy and displaced ones
without housing, security, permanence
many living in cars.

Regrouping, leaders announce
adjusted hours, offerings, services, provisions.
They arrange for gravel, cinders, pallets
all donated
a community effort to get evacuees up or off
the too-often-wet ground.

Aloha and unity permeate attitudes
of the *Puna* district and beyond.
Pu`u Honua `O Puna
still distributes donations
of food, clothing, bedding, provisions.
The community responds generously, heartily.

Residents and evacuees
celebrate the leaders and volunteers
who built the Hub, urgently
with intention and care
who quickly organized
arranged for construction and donations
who tried to arrange shelters
and housing for families
quickly erecting tiny houses
for singles, the elderly, the sick.

Churches and organizations
step up to help
offer space, services, hope.

Road volunteers contribute
time, labor, equipment
open an escape route
with giant tractors and expertise
along a previous lava flow
from *Pu`u `Ō`ō*.

That prior eruption
covered the highway
destroyed *Kalapana*.

Today, many generously and selflessly
donate time, energy, and imagination!

Thanks to *kanaka maoli* culture
aloha lives in *Puna,* but like everywhere
there is looting and drug violence.

Will the eruption end soon?
Will the Hub of activity close?
Will service still thrive?
No comment, no answer.

The Hub and Company

Online, I connect with evacuees and helpers
at the *Pu`u `O Honua `O Puna* Hub.
I join virtual community groups
"*Puna Lava Updates*" and "*Hawai`i Tracker.*"

We are eager to get the daily volcano analysis
predictions and possible consequences.
Residents report to the world
from the danger zone.
I witness, I question, I write.

My cyberspace friends include
the founder of the Hub, *Ikaika Marzo*
who pilots the *Kalapana Cultural Tours.*
Via video, I ride his lava boat
some early mornings and evenings
or go on paw walks near homes by the flow.

Everyone feels at home with scientists like
Philip Ong called "Dr. Phil" and other experts
who observe the developing conditions.
I fly along in deafening helicopters
with Scott and Bruce
who observe changes, breakouts
unstoppable paths of the boiling red river.

The Gathering Place

The Hub began at the beginning phase
of the eruption, a brainstorm, a foresight
fulfilling an urgent and immediate need
helping evacuees, residents, family, visitors
all without means or will to flee the scene.

It was an inspired plan for community support
envisioned by *Ikaika Marzo*
survivor of the *Kalapana-Kapoho* eruptions
a fisherman, surfer, tour leader, and musician
and his fearless team, tight like family
who gathered together and coalesced
around the threatened communities
and continuing evacuations.

The Hub used a donated empty lot
and became a gathering place
offered hope and shelter
for the shocked and dispossessed residents
provided donations: groceries, cooked meals
gas masks, supplies, tents, bottled water
personal items, bedding, toiletries, pet food.

It included space and corners
for government services and advice
FEMA, insurance reps, counselors
compassionate support at the one-stop Hub
under fiery skies and uncertainty.

Three months later
the team of volunteers
prepared to reorganize
improve the parking and sleeping areas
cut back on services and hours
where alternative solutions had been found.
Daily updates continued reliably
by Phil, *Ikaika*, John, Ken, Bruce, Scott, Dane
Dave, Jason, Ryan, Harry, Nathan, Dallas
and a growing group of many others.

The motto, "Stay Strong, Stay Classy, *Puna*,"
echoed like an affirmation.
The Hub`s gang of leaders, volunteers, and
experts repeated it regularly.

The media and the virtual world watched
as newly mentored assistants stepped up
took the baton, and shared.
The *LERZ* community and beyond
salute the leadership at the Hub!

The Hub and Sky

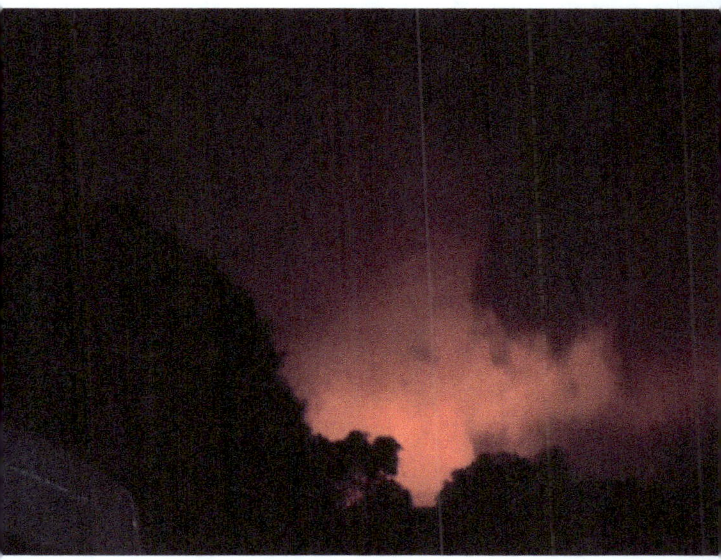

Uncertain in *Puna*

Island life goes on daily
familiar and secure
except in *Puna*
where communities struggle to survive
at the Hub and other shelters.

People wonder what is more authentic
than *Nature*'s power?

Residents on site take a rocky ride around
slippery lava fields
experience technological wonders
and social media
feel unpredictable about the nature of reality
uneasily creeping out and down
threatening like the volcano
their emotions bumping along like the
undulating rivers of lava.

Lava Drama

Contrapuntal rain
pours down on *Puna* again.
Fissure 8 surges dramatic
spillovers, breakouts
breathing waves and pulses of heat.

Pele's volatile rhythms and patterns
begin to unveil their mysteries.
Significant lava ponding spreads out eerily.
Hot lounging gathering pools turn dangerous
as islands rise and fall on beat with explosions
contrapuntal collapses, *Halema`uma`u* crater.

Unpredictable situations arise hour to hour
with whimsical, temperamental *Pele*.
Everyone remains on alert, vulnerable.
Cinderland, Papaya Farms, Noni Farms Road
threatened but still spared? Uncertainties.

After a change in direction, lava picks up
And a new channel forms and deepens.

Massive, towering pressure
pushes the dangerous flow
forcibly down fresh pathways to the sea.

Another Week

Despairing residents and evacuees hang on
instability, variability, up-rift.

Unpredictable dormant fissures awaken
menace still-standing homes
in *Leilani Estates* and beyond.
Multiple changes lift residents higher
into awe, fear, and hope.

They observe new eruption phases
road blocks, fallen tree barriers
unstable cliffs of towering lava.
Official barricades block access
to affected or threatened areas
highways cracking, sumping, dangerous.
Fines and arrest warrants are activated
for homeowners on their own private property
for outsiders and anyone caught
viewing or recording the lava
too hot and too close.

What's going on? What's happening?
Frustration grips; laws contradict reality.

Pressure and Patterns

Fissure 8 smokes deep down
diminishes reserves, empties lava.
Pressure patterns of eruptions
remain erratic, irregular, unstable.

Volcanic activity is unpredictable
when *Pele* comes around.
Fickle, she pauses, slowly drains *Fissure 8*
and it trickles down to the ocean entrance.

At the Hub, volcanic vibrations become harder
for experts to interpret and predict.
Does movement still crack the ground?

Lava and fissures slowly settle all around
after a vigorous, terrifying three months.

Meanwhile new observations:
Another crater known as *Pu`u `Ō`ō*
that had been asleep begins belching.
Rumors also abound of new movement
in the giant *Mauna Loa* nearby.

How much can we know and understand?

Catching Up

More road closures on the horizon
larger, important connectors uncertain
changing conditions expose lack of knowing.

Acidic rain storms, flood alerts, and advisories
pour in and swirl in *Puna*, off balance.
We listen to the crackling
the crumbling approaching *a`a*
rushing thick frightening sounds of lava rivers.
All around, gardens, wild grass, and leaves die.
Trees fall. Cracks grow.
We see the creative work of *Madame Pele*
visible and invisible.

Night singing *coqui* frogs fill the red silence.

Will pressure erupt in another place?

Dinner in *Pāhoa*

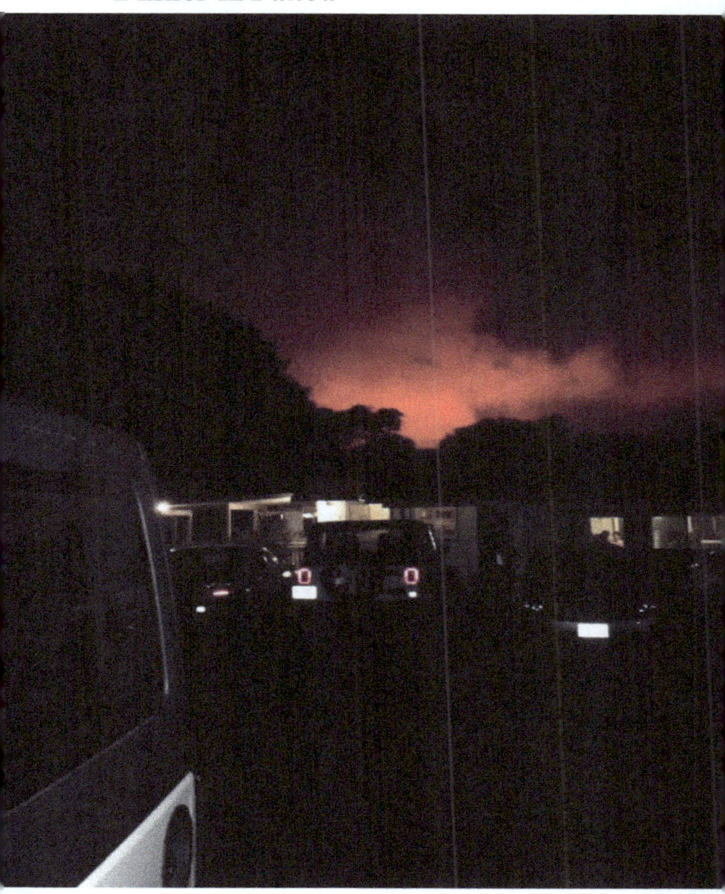

Respite

Puna is beyond the edge of endurance.

The residents, reporters, pilots
walking warriors
volunteers, tour guides
Civil Defense authorities
are exhausted yet awake
to the continuing uncertainty
sustained by the new silver threads
of connection and friendships.

People remain confused
by worrisome pictures, writing, reports.
To relieve stress, they connect
through the Hub, shelters, social media.
Emotions are balanced
by music, art, and *pa`ina* gatherings.

On site, meetings, collaborations, questions
and answers . . . sometimes
provide interpretation of overwhelming events.

FEMA, Civil Defense, National Guard
insurance firms, legal services give support.

Volunteers help distraught people and animals.

In the crisis, there was a respite in the flow.
The pause in eruptions
stunned the public, their relief palpable.

Many begin to smile
visit together, gather and relax
for a few minutes, or hours.
Folks begin to enjoy once again
vibrant sunsets, a meal, a shower, a good sleep
until . . . the next phases of the unknown.

Some residents have already moved away
monetarily secure, happy to be free
of the tumultuous uncertainty.

Those who remain gather strength
in preparation for whatever comes next.
Can it get any worse?

The Farmers' Market

Highway 130 is open again
leading to the Farmers' Market.
Tarps are up.
Vendors, friends, and neighbors
eccentric and ordinary people
greet one another warmly
rejoice to take the ride down the hill
to the acre of stalls opened early
finally accessible again.

Open Market Delights

On a Saturday drive down the hilly road
around the open market in lower *Puna*
almost surrounded by fields of new lava
we discover fruits, vegetables, exotic plants
fresh-cooked foods, handcrafted apparel
bric-à-brac, Hawaiian prints and patterns.

Puna is a vegetarian's paradise
inspiring special exotic recipes:
varieties of mangos and sweet melons
bananas, papayas, pineapples
dragon fruits, delightful avocados
lettuces, tomatoes, cucumbers
bunches of hearty greens and broccoli
colorful squashes, bitter melons, bell peppers
eggplants of all shapes and sizes
cabbages, potatoes, garlics
onions—green, big and yellow, red and purple
turmeric, ginger, rosemary, thyme, oregano
cocoa, vanilla beans, coffee, and beloved tea.

There are health foods, preserved chutneys
baked `*ōhana* cookies, coconut cakes
haupia and *kūlolo* puddings
concoctions with medicinal qualities
and orchids, anthuriums, haleconias
creative arts and crafts displayed
in colorful homemade clothes, tie-dyes.
Abundant organic market reopens to delight.

Plants and People

At the market, flowers are unimaginable
bouquets and pots of magical orchids
anthuriums, gingers, and *ōlena* turmeric
a miscellaneous section with potted plants
known and unknown to the garden novice.

Other stalls offer yard-sale items
hot-food specials, plate lunches.
Picnic benches are set up to gather and eat
under tarps and military-issue protection.

People pause, visit, share, and update others
on the volcano situation and new gossip
eruption consequences and ramifications
in their various neighborhoods
before returning home, happy and fortified
to face and confront
the ongoing uncertainty and lurking fears.

Part V

Awe and Beauty

Cloud Hues

Tall clouds, puffy whites, dirty browns
greatening grays, purples, and even charcoal
become familiar.

Clouds morph in speed and tones.
Silent spectacles surprise.

Shape-shifters paint the evening.
Clouds crawl then dash across the sky
symbiotic with the volcano's fluctuations
unpredictable.

Nightly tall thick clouds near *Fissure 8* radiate
incandescent colors
astound small humans who observe colorful
changes in the moon's path.

Below the clouds, survival of communities is
unknown and uncertain.

New Directions

Surprise new birth!

The eruption creates realistic possibilities
alongside ghost homes and the homeless.

Fire meets water, transforms, nurtures hope
visible and invisible seeds of creativity.

From out-of-pattern events
inspiration, imagination, and innovation
grow and flow exponentially, give birth to art.

Pele's flare-ups may cook burning destruction
but she stirs inertia, boils spicy possibilities
and crafts dark despair into mysterious art.

Her art blossoms into forms and color.

Moving forward again?

Closer and Closer

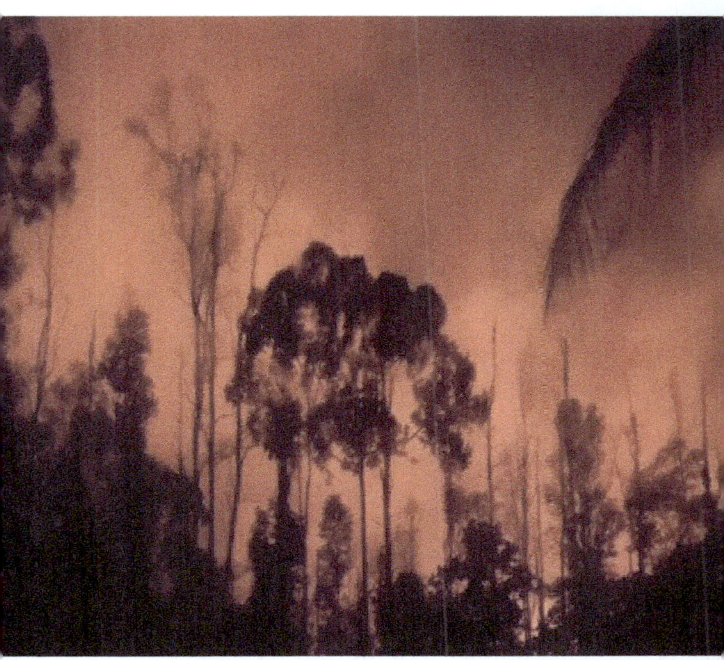

Lava River

Visions, vermillion plumes rise and fall
splashed with orange and iridescent blues
dancing in abandon.
The red planet Mars hangs
bright in the star-studded sky.

The lava river mirrors glowing moonbeams
meanders down its fiery path to presence
evokes human perceptions
of chaotic uncertainty
fluctuates, moves fast, then slowly
toward the beckoning summer sea.

Unexpected, sudden squalls and thunderstorms
cover the light, surprise the residents
as lingering effects
of passing summer storms, tropical depressions
fearsome dreams, and hurricanes.

Awesome, falling from the ghostly *Puna* sky
unfamiliar tephra, olivine
feathery ash, bitter SO2.

What is the paradoxical lesson
to be learned of dreams and visions
during volcanic disaster
and traveling destruction?
How to think about service, the youth
and gargantuan environmental changes?
Who, what, how do we serve?

Pause. Breathe. Allow the flow to show.
Observe objectively.
Expand the distance of consciousness
to our planet.
Serve the processes of rebirth and growth
understand the powerful energy of destruction.

A full moon chant blooms
inside the visionary mind.
Emotional realization of holy presence.

"I am open. I have enough. I am enough."
Mmmm. Ommm. Huuuu . . . .

Pele and Dance

Flame symphony of *Fissure 8*
excites the senses.

Lava tunes of reds, oranges, yellows
purples, grays, blacks
staccato stanzas of leaping crimson plumes
colorful clouds drum to crescendo
across western skies
at spreading ocean entries.

Pele dances at *Fissure 8*.
Photos capture mirages of a beautiful woman
reveal illusive images, myths enlivened
embellished, repeated, oral tradition
imagined memory of her *hula*
choreographed swaying, dipping, enticing
sensual `ami and kaholo*.

She unveils her awesome likeness
pictured phantasms in the sacred fire-river.

Beguiling seekers, *Pele* is a holy dancer
in the bewitching beams of sacred night.

Puna Update

Whew!

Respite, great feeling of relief
An interlude eases in to precious duration
long or short?

The fiery plume seems to be mysteriously
diminishing into a slow, dramatic act.

Last night, *Pele*'s lava river dried up.

Today
almost no eruptions
noticeable earthquakes, forced evacuations
in the *Lower East Rift Zone* in *Puna*
fewer toxic fumes, gases, scary rumblings
less dread to invade the sinus of nerves.

At the Hub, the tilt plot reveals
diminishing lava movement in the core
reflects mostly a decline, deflation
measureable emptying of lava.

Yesterday
Hurricane Hector hurried past
as a tropical storm
moving south, leaving mild effects:
blustery winds, flooding rains
frightening lightning and thunder
creating ponds, runoff all around
nurturing many new black sand beaches
and hope.

Soon, residents will again celebrate
blue skies, clear air
dramatic, colorful sunsets
along the coastline
lavender evenings, cool breezes
star-flung nights.
People are hopeful and smiling
anticipating that the worst is over.

Imagine, rejoice in a coming peace
for *Hawai`i Island.*

Not Unexpected

Amazing activities, eruptions, reactions
multiply on a largish island
situated in the Pacific ring of fearsome fire
and volcanic surprises.

Daily, black sand beaches
appear and disappear
like people, like floods, like politics.
Treasured tide pools are devoured
by 40+ foot walls of lava.

Explosions create lethal *laze*
where mountainous flows meet the ocean
building acres upon acres of new land.

We witness and verify a changing planet
subjected to expansionist greed and abuse
plastic and debris
in spite of frowns, fears, tears
illusions of safe, yet paranoid people
created in fake news.

Trickster Security

In early May, the *Puna* district
hoped for green expectancy of summer joy.

Laughing together
people shared fruits and flowers
a mutual sense of hope and harmony.

The new day revealed
towering movements of heat
dry, burning, red energy overwhelming all.

Surprise lava channels
filled cracks and crevices
spilled over tall black walls.
A relentless fire flow destroyed
tropical greenery, orchards, and native forests.

Overnight, the lava river crusted over
on the way down the mountain
to the ocean entrance.
The chickens and other birds all fell silent.

After the eruption
the surviving birds, owls, and small life
slowly returned
to burned branches
acres and miles of blight.

From May to August 2018
peaceful reality changed:
the trickster of destruction and regeneration
arrived on the scene.

The miracle—
new land and green growth emerged.

Children with forever altered hearts
lamented lost lands and homes
leaving red memories of *Nature*'s wonders.

Flyovers

Dedicated to updates, residents are respectful
awed by *Pele*'s undeniable power.

Photographers, volcanologists, tourists
hire small planes and helicopters
discover craters, flows, burning homes
surrounded by impassable lava.

Videos share a more objective picture
from a heightened perspective.

Noisy flyovers intruding into the peaceful sky
at least twice daily observe and report
about the thrilling vagina of boiling *Fissure 8*.

Drones, mostly illegal, sneak in, and report.

Attentive to changing conditions
residents, animal lovers, and pilots
search for stranded animals to rescue.

To ease anxiety, residents share information
grateful for the gift of beautiful, sacred land.

Awe in *Pāhoa*

Gratitude

Celebrate! Generosity and *aloha* spirit
compassion, shared experiences, and growth.

Folks at the Hub work long hours
and keep the public informed.

Volunteers especially *kūpuna*
help the evacuees and their families.

Volcanologists, geologists, naturalists
writers, artists, musicians
provide data and support
along with boat and helicopter pilots.

There is also walking, filming, commenting
by displaced residents called "Road Warriors."

Rejoice! The volcano's legacy is survival.
Puna will overcome disaster and rebuild.

Honor! Friends ordinary and extraordinary.

Good Imperatives

Learn and digest Hawaiian myths and legends
the personal experiences behind
complex changing headlines and forecasts.

Experience the science:
earthquakes, tsunamis, eruptions, types of lava
cracks in the earth and poisonous emissions.

Resist, expose greedy corporate complicity—
building subdivisions on an active rift zone
setting up buyers for failure
known and unknown.

In the face of destructive forces
remember to bow
to the intoxicating beauty of creation.

Scales of Memory

Recall volunteers, cooks, reporters, friends
USGS park rangers and representatives of land
on site agencies like *FEMA*
health and legal experts.
Acknowledge donations
incredible animal rescues
(dogs, cats, horses, cattle, turtles, and more).

Observe the diminishing eruption
from 24 fissures to one
the slowing of the 2,000-degree+ lava river.
Marvel at the developing patterns
of breakouts discovered
using predictability models, technology.
Appreciate the finally foreseeable surges
from *Fissure 8*
the violent movement
occurring two hours after
each summit explosion
the pulses of lava
reoccurring every five minutes!

Picture the flows and erosion
the troublesome closures
of driveways, roads, and highways.
Witness the breathing eruption
changing like life itself.
Remember repetitive, miraculous
marvelous laws
governing *Nature*'s preeminent power
and give thanks.

Daily Miracles

The original horizon-scape is altered
by impossible passages, barren trees
burnt foliage, decimated flowers
ravaged gates and driveways of dead homes.

Ash-covered *Nature* and new *pu`u* cones
reveal blockages and open space
from the summit of *Mauna Kea* to the sea.

New vistas open to another beauty
the large awesome sky
no longer hidden by jungles of *Nature*
precious star-diamonds and moonrise
in the infinite bowl of night above.

Freeing thoughts beckon the observer
to be still, taste patience
in the moment to evaluate.

Past mysteries wink in the clear glow of now.
Choices and possibilities manifest
in empty spaces. Stay or leave?

The eruption nourishes vibrant being
births strength and humility.

We tremble on an ancient stage
play roles of faith, creation, and growth.

How to decide which way to turn and move
closer or not?
Toward or away from the fire
and adventure of the unknown?

Essence of Spirit shimmers.

Survivors

Pohoiki and *PGV* were still standing
until the last phase of the eruption.

Pohoiki (*Isaac Hale Beach Park*)
an ancient fishing port
and clean swimming place
traditionally refreshed and nurtured the locals.
Pohoiki was finally overtaken by lava
but the lagoon and sandbar reformed.
Fishermen, surfers, and families have returned.

Miracle!
The black sand beach splashed with olivine
sparkles once more under the tropical sun.

PGV (Puna Geothermal Venture)
a relatively new arrival on the island
was rumored to have been fracking
disturbing the Earth's inner core
while searching for alternative volcanic energy
fracking allegedly causing health issues
near the site, and possibly *Pele*'s eruption.

Due to encroaching lava
the company had to prepare and close down
but expects to reopen
as a source of energy
by the end of 2019
culpable or not.

In August at the end, the cracks retreated
and the flow slowed down.
The lava congealed. The air cleared.
People helped, let go of fears and negativity
and healed.
Survivors woke up to the act of letting go
embraced blue oceans of present needs
abandoned blame and pain, forgave grudges.

The leaders still remind us
"Stay Strong, Stay Classy, *Puna.*"
Go deep. Move on. Walk good.
Transformation is real and happening in *Puna.*
Hallelujah!

Evening in *Pāhoa*

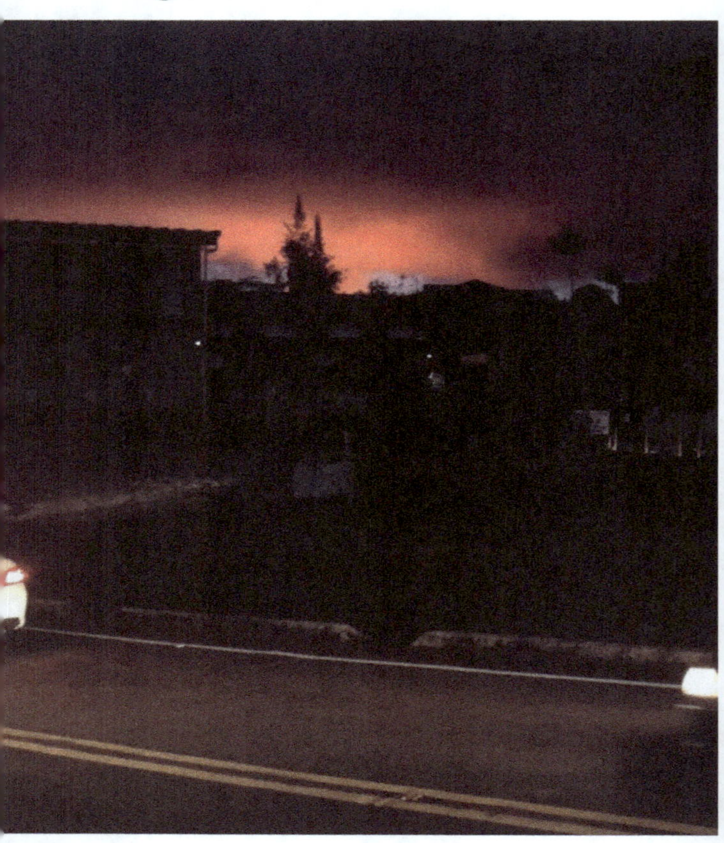

Volcano Consciousness

Go bravely
Plunge deep into the darkness
of an unexplored lava tube.
Decide how to be or not to be!
Question how to change
Now to drink our crystallized tears?
Emerge with clarifying answers.
Transform body, mind, and spirit
in a baptism by fire.

But what is the process?
Question the *kūpuna.*
Wake up to new realities
changed horizons of possible paths.

Residuals.
A deep pit of fiery primal fears
lurks within each
hidden or not.
Eruption is a metaphor.
Catch and melt the old in a new light.
Can we accept solutions
and then let our obstacles go?
Perennial inquiries and tastes
for answers persist.

Back Home

Five days after my departure
from *Hilo, Hawai`i*
I sit and stare at the jade trees
lining the familiar golden shores
of *Windward O`ahu.*

I arise and pick seven
heart-shaped, sea-grape leaves
from a mature tree at *Malaekahana*
a tableau upon which I can write
an outline of my story, our story
and dedicate a poem to you.

I lie down beneath the large shade
of a stand of towering eucalyptus trees
sensing clarity in the jade leaves above.
I hear a waterfall behind the nearby stream.

I delight in green and blue breezes
and homey possibilities of promising growth
reflecting on the fiery disruptions
experienced during the eruption
still in *Puna.*

Residents begin to recover and rebuild
struggle with authorities and bureaucracies.
I witness and remember the stages
of change and growth, corruption and healing.

I feel more comfortable
and relatively accepting
of the processes of destruction
and regeneration
happening a mere one-hour plane ride
over the omnipresent Pacific
from *Hilo* to *Honolūlū*.

I wonder about the difference
between voluntary and involuntary suffering.
A pebble of intention can transform hardship
into an esoteric promise of new beginnings.

Changing Conditions

Dropping into awareness
I feel a thread of light
across the red
horizon of my third eye.
I refocus, make new aims
commitments to create
and accept new situations
consequences of choice, or not.

**What tools can we use to save
our sacred values and principles?
What and where are the best questions
to ask, and to whom?**

I pause, clap my hands into the now
remember and observe changing conditions:
terrifying speeds, spillages
of raw searing heat.

Volunteer firefighters sweat profusely
driving tractors and backhoes
using picks and shovels to create a fire line
stop aggressive flames
melting the beloved `*āina.*

**How to drop into body
observe the mind and emotions?**

Volcanic eruptions are unstoppable
hot, crimson danger.
No choice but to allow lava
to flow and burn all in the path to completion.
I observe the subtle and blatant surges
of heat flowing, slowing to cool aqua peace.

Sacred or Not?

On the edge of self-transformation
missing balance
the nightly ritual of remembering
danger and safety.
Above, the moon waxes and wanes.
Another cycle of passages begins again.
Political suicide hovers, pervasive as tragedy.
Residents' complaints and pain double
to increase spectacle of enormous loss.
Cherished words of freedom and democracy
seem obsolete and forgotten.
The bully-full government takes control
dispensing disaster funds, or not.
Conflicts surge among local, state, and federal
assistance during emergency conditions
while personal rights and good decisions
burn and melt in remote offices.
Intensity of the unknown
heats essence essential.
Carnelian impressions camouflage
Pele's mysterious veil.
Slippery responses, excuses, abuses, failures
of enchanting eruption
elude reality.
What is sacred and not?

Kūpuna Songs

Remember insightful *kūpuna* lessons
unfolding in chanted stories.

Fearlessly seize adventures in bold harmonies.

Build sacred self
using tourmaline experiences and memories.

Share with the children.

Speak to those who question
life's rhythmic mysteries.

Clarity twinkles in a rainy peridot sky.

Musical voices of wisdom
ring the unknown yet perennial.

Scales of understanding silently rotate.

Just beyond the border of carnelian lava
true listening surpasses mere hearing.

Glossary

This glossary provides only brief definitions for terms. Please consult additional sources for further information.

A`a – Viscous lava flow whose surface is covered by thick, jumbled piles of loose, sharp rocks and blocks.

Ahalanui Beach Park – A Hawai`i Island beach park, which formerly had volcanically heated ponds.

Ahalanui Warm Ponds – Hot springs destroyed by lava in the 2018 eruption.

Ahu `Ai Lā`au – A Volcanic cone located near Fissure 8 on Hawai`i Island.

`Ai Lā`au – Hawaiian volcano god who devoured organic life. Also called the Forest Eater. Said to have gifted his sacred place in Halema`uma`u to Pele.

`Aina – Land, earth.

Aloha – Love, affection, compassion, greetings, hello, goodbye.

`Ami – A *hula* dance step/move.

Beach Lots, aka Kapoho Beach Lots – On July 4, 2018, the Hawaiian Volcano Observatory reported lava flowing into the ocean in the Kapoho area, destroying the Kapoho Beach Lots and Four Corners neighborhoods.

Big Island – Nickname for Hawai`i Island.

The Blue House – A landmark large home perched on a hill familiar to residents, which aids navigation in the ocean below the LERZ.

Bowls – A popular surf spot on Hawai`i Island in Pohoiki, which was destroyed during the 2018 eruption.

Campbell Pond – A pond in the LERZ that was destroyed by the 2018 lava flow.

Cheshire Cat – A character in the 1865 novel *Alice's Adventures in Wonderland* by British author Charles Lutwidge Dawson under the pen name Lewis Carroll. Alice falls into a garden rabbit hole and finds herself trapped in a world of fantastic creatures, including the Cheshire Cat. The Cheshire Cat continually smiles in face of danger and obliteration.

Cinderland EcoVillage – A three-acre tropical off-the-grid food farm on Hawai`i Island affected by the 2018 volcanic eruption.

Coqui – The common coquí is a tiny frog known for its loud, irritating chirps for mating at night, especially on Hawai`i Island.

Farmers' Almanac – The annual Farmers' Almanac since 1792 that includes weather, astronomy, astrology, gardening, planting, and harvesting information.

FEMA – The Federal Emergency Management Agency is an agency of the United States Department of Homeland Security, which helps victims of natural disasters.

Fissure 8 – One of 24 fissures in the LERZ, the only one that spilled continuous lava flows during the 2018 eruption.

Fissure 22 – One of 24 fissures in the LERZ.

Four Corners – On July 4, 2018, the Hawaiian Volcano Observatory reported lava flowing into the ocean in the Kapoho area, destroying the Kapoho Beach Lots and Four Corners neighborhoods.

Green Mountain – Located in the area of Kapoho, which is now uninhabited due to the 2018 volcanic eruption, this mountain is on the east end of the Kīlauea rift zone and the eastern tip of the Puna district and Hawai`i Island. It is said to be where each morning the sun first meets land in the Hawaiian islands.

Halema`uma`u – A pit crater located within the much larger summit caldera of Kīlauea in Hawai`i Volcanoes National Park.

Hale – Hawaiian word for house or home.

Haupia – A Hawaiian dessert made with coconut.

Hawai`i – The 50th state of the United States.

Hawaiian Acres – A mostly off-the-grid subdivision right above the LERZ near Kurtistown.

Hawai`i Island – Largest island in the Hawaiian group. Also called the Big Island.

**Hawai`i nei** – Literally, "Hawai`i here." The word *nei* gives a feeling of closeness.

Hawai`i Tracker – A community-based group on Facebook with an extensive audience during the 2018 eruption.

**Hawai`i Volcanoes National Park** – Established in 1916, this national park on Hawai`i Island encompasses two active volcanoes, Kīlauea and Mauna Loa.

**Hi`iakaikapoliopele** – Hawaiian goddess. Sister of Pele. Often abbreviated as Hi`iaka.

Hilo – The largest town in the district of Puna.

Honolūlū – Capital city of the State of Hawai`i.

Honua – Hawaiian word for land, earth, world.

Hui – A group formed in Hawai`i based on economic support and sharing resources.

Hula – Hawaiian dance performed by men and women usually accompanied with an *oli* or chant that often tells stories of genealogy, love, war, and legends.

Huna – Hawaiian word for hidden secret; hidden.

Ibiza – Imported tall tree, up to 80 feet. Modifies forest habitat by significantly increasing nitrogen levels in the soil, which makes the area inhospitable to native plants, but more suitable for other invasive species.

Ikaika – A Hawaiian name meaning strong, powerful, sturdy, strength, force, energy, might.

Ikaika Marzo – Native Hawaiian founder of Pu`u Honua `O Puna, the community Hub during the 2018 eruption. He is a community leader, entertainer, and tour boat pilot. He is also recognized as a local philosopher.

Isaac Hale Beach Park – On Hawai`i Island, a beach park in the Pohiki area that was overrun by lava in the 2018 volcanic eruption.

Jaggar Museum – Now-closed Hawai`i Island museum that was severely damaged in the 2018 volcanic eruption. Named after Thomas Augustus Jaggar (1871-1953), an early volcanologist who founded the Hawaiian Volcano Observatory.

Ka`a`awa – A small community in the Ko`olauloa district on the northeastern shore of O`ahu.

**Kahalū`u** – A community in the Ko`olaupoko district on the northeastern shore of O`ahu.

Kaholo – The "vamp" *hula* step, more common in modern than in ancient dance, consisting of four counts.

Kai – Hawaiian word for sea water.

Kaholo – A *hula* dance step/move.

Kalapana – Town and region in the Puna district of Hawai`i Island.

Kalapana Cultural Tours –A tour company out of Hilo with the boat piloted by Ikaika Marzo.

Kalapana-Kapoho – The 1955 volcanic and 2002 eruptions on Hawai`i Island affected these areas.

Kanaka maoli – Person of Native Hawaiian descent. People of the land.

Kapoho Village – Destroyed by the 2018 volcanic eruption, a now-uninhabited unincorporated area in the Puna district of Hawai`i Island.

Kapoho Tide Pools – Tide pools in the Kapoho areas that were celebrated for their beauty before their destruction in the 2018 volcanic eruption.

**Ka`u** – Southernmost district of Hawai`i Island.

Kaua`i – A northern Hawaiian island.

Kīlauea – Kīlauea is an active volcano in the Hawaiian islands. It is a shield volcano. The Hawaiian name Kīlauea means "spewing" or "much spreading."

Kilauea Iki – Literally, "Small Kīlaua." A pit crater next to the main summit, Kīlauea.

Kona – Abbreviated name for Kailua-Kona, a town on the west coast of Hawai`i Island.

Kua O Ka Lā – A charter school focused on Hawaiian language and culture destroyed in the 2018 volcanic eruption.

Kūlolo – A pudding made of baked or steamed grated taro and coconut cream.

Kupukupu – Native Hawaiian sword fern.

Kūpuna – In Hawaiian culture, a senior elder.

Lava Tree State Park – Located on Pāhoa-Pohoiki Road 2.7 miles southeast of Pāhoa in the Puna district of Hawai`i Island, this park is also known as Lava Tree State Monument.

Laze – Volcanic haze.

Leilani – Literally, "necklace of the heavens." A common Hawaiian given name.

Leilani Estates – Subdivision in the Puna district located in the Lower East Rift Zone (LERZ) on the Big Island of Hawai`i.

LERZ – Lower East Rift Zone, an area on Hawai`i Island prone to volcanic eruptions.

**Lohi`au** – A young chief from Kaua`i who was a renowned singer and Pele`s lover.

Mahealani – Sixteenth day of lunar month in the Hawaiian calendar. Night of a full moon.

Mahina – Hawaiin word for moon, moonlight. Hawaiian lunar goddess.

Malaekahana – Quiet bay and beach area south of Kahuku on the island of O`ahu.

Malulani Circle – According to *Ulukau: The Hawaiian Electronic Library*, Malulani is the name of one of the stars in the southern sky, conveying a divine presence. This street in Pāhoa on Hawai`i Island was affected by the 2018 volcanic eruption.

Mana – In Hawaiian culture, a spiritual energy of supernatural, divine, or miraculous power.

Mauna Loa – One of six volcanoes on Hawai`i Island.

Mauna Kea – One of six volcanoes on Hawai`i Island.

Mokihana – A small, leathery, cube shaped, anise-scented fruit, which changes from green to brown. They are often strung in *lei*. Many are found in the mountains of Kaua`i.

Nanawale – Subdivision near Pāhoa on Hawai`i Island; the name of a forest reserve.

Nature – All the plants, animals, and things existing in the universe that are not made by people.

Naupaka – In Hawai`i, a native species of jade-green shrubs found in mountains and near coasts, conspicuous for their white or light-colored flowers that look like half flowers. Hawaiian legend of two lovers separated.

Noni Farms Road – Road in the Puna district of Hawaii Island affected by the 2018 volcanic eruption. The *noni* plant is the India mulberry, a small tree or shrub in the coffee family.

**O`ahu** – The most populous of the Hawaiian Islands and the seat of Honolūlū, the capital city of the State of Hawai`i.

`Ōhana – Family, relatives, kin group.

`Ōhi`a lehua – Endemic to Hawai`i, flowering evergreen tree in the myrtle family that has delicate red flowers called *lehua*. One of the first trees that grows out of newly formed lava.

Olena – Turmeric, a kind of ginger distributed from India into Polynesia.

Pahala – Town in the Puna district, southwest of Hawai`i Island.

Pāhoa – Village near Leilani Estates on Hawai`i Island.

Pahoehoe – Basaltic lava forming smooth undulating or ropy masses.

Papaya Farms Road – Located in Pāhoa on Hawai`i Island, this road was affected by the 2018 volcanic eruption.

Pa`ina – In Hawaiian culture, meal, dinner, small supper party.

**Pala`ā** – Fine lace fern native to Hawai`i.

Palapalai – Rigid lace fern native to Hawai`i.

Pele – Hawaiian goddess of volcanoes. Also known colloquially as "Madame Pele."

Pohoiki – Coastal land section in the LERZ area of Hawai`i Island. Popular fishing site and pier used by locals until it was destroyed by the 2018 volcanic eruption.

PGV – A company on Hawai`i Island called Puna Geothermal Ventures. Public protests alleged that its emissions caused illnesses.

Puna – A district on the southeast side of Hawai`i Island.

Puna Lava Updates –A virtual group on Facebook visited by people around the world following the 2018 eruption.

**Punalu`u** – A beach area in Puna on Hawai`i Island.

Pu`u – Volcanic cones.

Pu`u Honua `O Puna – The community Hub in Pāhoa on Hawai`i Island.

**Pu`u `Ō`ō** – Vent in Hawai`i Volcanoes National Park that erupted continuously from 2002 until 2018, just before the 2018 eruption in the Lower East Rift Zone.

The Red House – A landmark house for community events at Pohoiki.

Secrets – A popular surf spot, near Pohoiki on Hawai`i Island, which was destroyed during the 2018 volcanic eruption.

Shacks – A surf spot popular with locals in Pohoiki, affected by the 2018 eruption.

South Point – Also known as Ka Lae, this area is the southernmost point of Hawai`i Island and of the United States.

Strawberry Moon – A Native American term for the full moon in June, so named because wild berries start to ripen at that time.

Tiare – A Tahitian ginger bush/small tree.

USGS – The United States Geological Survey, a scientific agency of the federal government. Its scientists study and monitor land, natural resources, and natural hazards. During the 2018 eruption in Hawai`i, the USGS provided daily updates.

Vacationland – Also called Kapoho Vacationland, this area was a coastal subdivision in Kapoho on Hawai`i Island.

Vog – A form of air pollution that results when sulfur dioxide and other gases and particles emitted by an erupting volcano react with oxygen, moisture, and sunlight.

Volcano House – A hotel located at the edge of Kīlauea Volcano inside the grounds of Hawai`i Volcanoes National Park. It houses the Volcano Arts Center. Between May and October 2018, the hotel and the volcano's summit were closed due to volcanic activity.

Volcano Village – Near the Halema`uma`u and Kīlauea Iki craters, this village next to the Hawai`i Volcanoes National Park hosts locals and visitors interested in walking and hiking amid the volcanic landscape. The village was threatened by the 2018 volcanic eruption.

Wahine `Oma`o – Companion of Hi`iaka who accompanied her on her quest to bring Lohi`au back to Pele.

**Windward `Oahu** – Area from Waimānalo to Kahuku, noted for its trade winds, the Ko`olau mountain range, beautiful beaches, and lush green vegetation.

About the Author

Kathryn Waddell Takara, PhD, is a scholar, performance artist, and author of eight books of poetry, a biography, and a collection of oral 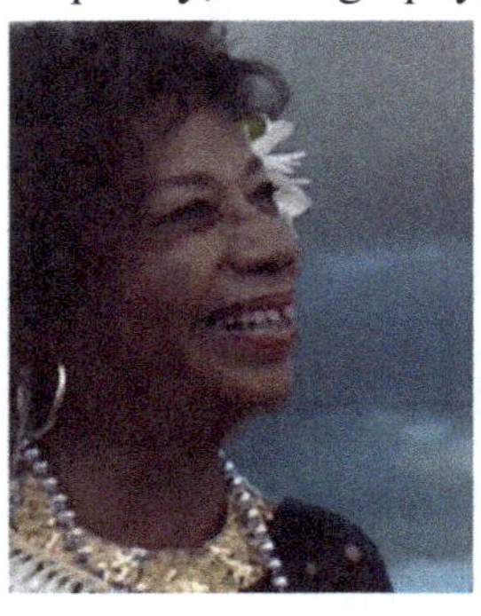 histories. The Before Columbus Foundation honored her in 2010 with the American Book Award. She has appeared on television and in documentary films, and frequently has given media and publication interviews. She publishes articles on culture, most recently in *The Black Chicago Renaissance* and *Black Hollywood Unchained*.

Born and raised in Tuskegee, Alabama, in the Jim Crow era, Takara is a longtime resident of Hawai`i. With an MA in French and a PhD in Political Science, until retiring as an Associate Professor, at the University of Hawai`i at Mānoa, she taught African American and African history, politics, literature, and culture, and organized conferences on minority issues.

Takara delivers lectures and performs her unique ethnic, travel, political, and eco-poetry across the United States and internationally. Notably, she has appeared in China at Qingdao University and Beijing University of Foreign Studies; Bordeaux, France; Abidjan, Côte d'Ivoire; and Niamey, Niger. In 2018-2019, she gave poetry readings in California, New York, and Virginia. She often shares her poetry with audiences in Hawai`i, including this year at the Paliku Arts Festival—and at a jazz event featuring the music of Thelonious Monk, which she co-produced.

She is the owner and publisher of Pacific Raven Press, LLC (established 2008), which has published 18 titles.

Personal experiences with the 2018 volcanic eruption on the Big Island of Hawai`i inspired Takara to write **_Red Dreams, Volcano Visions_**.

To order books, visit Pacific Raven Press:
www.pacificravenpress.co/
www.kathrynwaddelltakara.com